THE HUMAN MEANING

Valentin Matcas, M.Ed.

ISBN: 9781980780427

DEDICATION

I dedicate this book to everyone eager to learn and develop
continuously throughout life.

CONTENTS

1 THE HUMAN NEEDS AND MEANINGS, NATURAL AND CONSENSUAL

Love and the Divine are the best meanings there can be, just because love stands at the top of your feelings and you treasure it the most, while the Divine is everything that exists. You cannot find anything beyond love and the Divine capable enough to set your meaning in life and in this world, simply because there is nothing else beyond them.

However, there is significantly more to learn and understand about the human meaning, just because, as it is presented in this world today through science, literature, philosophy, and through the rest of ideologies, it is not enough. You fail to understand the human meaning, and this causes you to fail your own meaning in life and in this world, at least your natural meaning, as you receive it from Life and from the Divine. Because the concept of meaning is presented to you empirically today, you cannot understand it accurately in this manner but only through doctrine and beliefs, you can never engage your reasoning in this manner in order to grasp accurately your own natural meaning, your natural meaning is easily hijacked, and everything is done on purpose, to harm and exploit you. In this manner, you end up fulfilling consensually implemented meanings throughout life, on behalf of the rich and the powerful of this world, since they are the ones controlling ideologies and therefore consensual meanings in this world. Not much that you do now counts for Life and for the Divine, despite of what ideologies tell and promise, and when you look back, now you may see the kind of world that you create. And do not blame the rich and the powerful of this world, since you are the one doing everything, for them.

Many times, it is for your children that you struggle throughout life, to make them happy, to make them worthy, and to make everything count, because this is exactly your meaning in your family. Yet can't it be the same in your community and in society?

Does it ever make a difference to have or not to have a specifically defined meaning in life and in this world? Yes, it certainly makes a difference, because all meanings count, even the slightest ones, since they are connected. And it is always a matter of identifying your meanings instead of fulfilling them unknowingly, otherwise you end up working your entire life in vain. While through your consensually induced meanings, you end up working against the meanings of others, deliberately or not, living your life against your loved ones. While they can certainly feel, and this ruins entire relationships. This is your consensual meaning in your family, in society, in life, and in this world. And so you end up living your life against yourself, against your own natural meaning.

Throughout this book, we follow, identify, define, understand, and model the human meaning, genuine and consensual, from all perspectives and in all contexts. You learn about your meaning in life, in this world, in society, within your family and genetic line, within you own cognitive system, within higher worlds, and within everything that exists.

But how much do you know about meanings and purposes right now? People have already studied the meaning of life, and they found that the meaning of life, and consequently your meaning in life, is love. Love and the Divine again, since all you need is love. You must live your life in order to find love, while seeking the Divine. You find love in life, you share it with others, you give love, you find the Divine, you believe in the Divine and you serve the Divine, and this is exactly what life is, this is your meaning in life, and it is this simple. You give a big hug to all your loved ones every day, in the morning and in the evening before they go to bed, and this is what life is, this is your meaning in life and in this world. And now you know it well, because this must be the human meaning. Right?

Yes, certainly, and you already know all these, since there are countless of books and movies on this theme, love and the Divine. Yet there is something else involved here, since the meaning of everything in everything seems to be more complex and more significant. You cannot tell what it is, since there cannot be anything more meaningful and more important in life and in this world than love and the Divine, yet you can never pinpoint what it is, can you?

Because there is more to your meaning in life, in humanity, and in this world than love and the Divine. Yet it is also consistent with love and the Divine, as you cannot grasp it entirely, and therefore you cannot fulfill it. Because your own beliefs state that your current understanding of love and of the Divine is excellent and complete, just because your designated ideology claims to be excellent and complete itself, the best in this world, and the only one.

Well, but why exactly do you feel that there is more than love and the Divine to count and to be considered throughout this study of the human meaning? Because nothing that you find so far about the true human meaning is capable to show and explain to you the multitude of your needs, tendencies, instincts, thinking, and behavior, all leading consistently to a meaning yet to a meaning that is not exactly love and the Divine. Unlimited wealth, social supremacy, and material pleasure are but simple examples here, with each one exceeding by far your two meanings, love and the Divine. You might not want this to be your case, yet it is, for the simple fact that you use money and follow orders in society and throughout life, and these alone take you further away from

Life, from love, and from the Divine. You can do nothing about it, and this is why now your meaning in life might not be exactly what you expect and what you intend, love and the Divine.

What exactly is going on? All ideologies state clearly that it is your fault for not being capable to fulfill your meaning as they state, yet when you study this meaning closely, you find it consensually implemented in you, through ideological beliefs. This is a consensual meaning, and not your actual genuine human meaning. Yet many times, ideologies do not even allow you to reason and tell the difference, but only to follow their beliefs, exactly as stated. I am not referring only to social, political, national, or religious ideologies, since ideologies are everywhere and of all kind, hidden and in the open, legal and illegal, they count in tens of thousands by now and they always get to you, and so they invade your mind, your soul, your spirit, and your entire world. Science itself is an ideology today, along with education, religion, media, entertainment, spirituality, and even medicine, TV, and business, along with society entirely. They indoctrinate you by altering your meaning in life and in this world at its core, you fall for it since there is nothing else to consider, it happens to everyone, and this is the kind of environment that you now inhabit.

I refer to this altered, consensual environment as the Consensual Matrix. Because you always have one meaning for each environment to consider, as you have a natural, genuine meaning for each natural, genuine environment, always related to Life, love, and the Divine. While you have a consensual meaning for any of your consensual environments, related to the multitude of beliefs, ideologies, hierarchies, jobs, orders, hierarchic Brotherhood, assignments, slogans, consensuses, indoctrination, control, and slavery. While this is your Consensual Matrix, and this is how you live your life, mostly by fulfilling your consensual meaning. This is your meaning in life and in this world today, your human meaning, and when you look around and study it closely, you find it mostly consensual.

Yet this world never considers any of these, and it should.

While there is still more to add to this subject, since life is more complex. And you should be able to understand everything, or your ignorance drops you under servitude and control, with or without your knowledge. Because life is not as simple as you notice on TV, and this is why it takes this entire book and book series to find and explain the human meaning, in all its natures and forms, and from all perspectives.

While society with all its ideologies gives you a handful of rimes and slogans to use from now on as a meaning in life, and it is never enough to know and understand your true meaning in life and in this world. You cannot follow that handful of rimes, slogans, and beautiful words anyway, since they are empiric and ideal, mostly. You end up living your life differently and you are blamed for your entire behavior, not much of what you do in life in this manner makes sense and it lacks meaning, and you wish that you knew what is really going on.

And this is how you have two distinct choices right now, to keep this research of your human meaning genuine and unbiased, in order to find out what you do wrong the entire time and why you are failing your intelligent human meaning, if you happen to fail it. Or you may simply accept now that you are always good, since you never actually use money, power, pleasure, and people throughout life in any manner, regardless if this is true or not. Yet only the truth sets you free, since money, hierarchies, power, beliefs, lies, and influence are not at all about love and the Divine, while they make for plausible, important, useful meanings in life and in this world as you know, and everybody has them. And you can never have them both, you can never seek both natural meanings and consensual ones as money, drugs, servitude, and indoctrination, since your natural and consensual meanings are disjunctive, they enter in conflict many times, and this creates all problems that you have throughout life.

While your ideologies state clearly what meaning you should seek and fulfill, love and the Divine, or love, your nation, your brotherhood, or your political party, including or not the Divine, depending on your designated ideology, since these count by the hundreds of thousands, and they state that it is your fault in life every time you fail or avoid them. And it is not your fault, just because their beliefs enter in conflict with your own intrinsic, natural needs and meanings. And since all your conflicting meanings, natural and consensual, claim to seek love, righteousness, and many times the Divine, while they enter in even more conflict when you have additional meanings in life as wealth, power, supremacy, influence, lies, domination, and tribute, now it seems relevant to find out what exactly is going on, just because consensual beliefs shape and reshape your life many times for the worse, it happens to everybody while no one ever cares and it influences them for the worse, while they assume to be their fault.

First, you do not have only one designated ideology but a multitude, some identified and some not, some in the open and some hidden, some legal and some illegal. Yet regardless of the circumstance, all these ideologies are implemented and maintained implemented by your authorities, in the name of your authorities, regardless if they accept this to be the case or not, Life and the Divine send you your natural needs and meanings with your ideologies sending you your consensual needs and meanings. And natural and consensual meanings enter in conflict, because your needs stand at the base of your meanings. You may consider religious ideologies here, but these are not the only ones, since it is capitalism sending you needs related to money, wealth, supremacy, and material influence, and these define your meaning now. And with communism using money, wealth, and currencies, communism is capitalism in disguise. While all your needs, natural and consensual, stand at the base of your meanings, with your most powerful and persistent needs hijacking your meaning in life and in this world as they please, or as they are designed to do.

And this explains the conflict between your natural and consensual meanings, and it has your needs at its base, your natural and consensual needs. Because the fulfillment of your natural physiological needs enters in conflict with all your ideologies, and with justice itself, and many times with the entire society. And since justice and society constrain you through severe punishment to follow your consensual needs instead of your natural ones, you do so, and this explains your consensual life here as a human being. And this is why you will always fail your ideologies, not because you are incapable to follow their beliefs through lack of ability, but because it is designed to happen in this manner to you.

Yet there is more taking place, and you have to know everything in order to understand your meanings in life, both natural and consensual, since you happen to live your life at their confluence. And they will never leave you alone, but they will tear you apart, until they get what they want from you, your natural meaning, coming from Life and from the Divine, through the multitude of needs and feelings of your cognitive system. Along with your consensual meaning coming from your authorities and from those controlling your authorities, through the multitude of morals, laws, doctrine, orders, beliefs, and entire ideologies.

But why having the dreadful discrepancy between the intended, good human meaning in life, and the unwanted, commonly occurring consensual meaning in life? To give your answer right away, this happens because many people want to take advantage of you, they want to put you to work, exploit you, harvest you, use you, harm you, harvest and exploit this world through you, harm this world through you, exploit your soul and your entire higher self through you, and then take over your niche in life and in this world. While all these enter in conflict with what Life and the Divine want from you, since you are here to live your life naturally and to behave naturally, on their behalf.

And this circumstance is highly complex today, just because it has been going on for a very long time, almost eternally. While there are definite laws put in place to make order in everything, higher and lower laws, as they state clearly that no one may exploit, use, and harm you in any manner, and that you have all rights to live your life by fulfilling your natural needs and meanings, for Life and for the Divine. And this is exactly how your life should be. Yet it never happens in this manner, because every law may be twisted in every manner to make it state even the opposite if needed, to make you do the opposite and fall into slavery. Since this is why you have ended up with both natural and consensual meanings to fulfill throughout life, with all the tricks and shenanigans making everything happen, and coincidentally, with all these tricks and shenanigans abiding accurately to all laws, higher and lower.

How does everything happen and how can anyone ever be capable to infringe the higher laws? Yes, this is the question, since if it never happened, then you were free to fulfill your natural needs and meanings, alongside your loved ones. How does everything happen? You do everything. All those exploiting you are innocent, while you take the blame. You are the one infringing all laws, you are always the one eager to fulfill your consensual needs and meanings throughout life, to work for your authorities and for those controlling your authorities going in this manner against Life and the Divine. You state it clearly that you want to fall into servitude and to be harmed and exploited in any manner and you even sign for it. And no one can do anything about it now, because it is your choice to fulfill your consensual meaning throughout life. Everybody allows you to do so now since you insist, and so you do, for life.

Yet you might already know these, if you are from the Brotherhood. And you know everything, if you are from the Elite. I divide society in these three social classes, the Masses, the Brotherhood, and the Elite. Since in general, if you compete alone or within a small family throughout life and throughout this world, you are from the Masses. But if you compete in very large groups, legal or illegal, as business cartels, lodges, unions, congregations, mobs, business and financial clubs, gangs of all types, and political parties, you are from the Brotherhood, and you already know it. Since these work with each other while comprising the current hierarchic Brotherhood and exploiting this world, and then they share the profit. And they do everything on behalf of the Elite, which is the upper social class. Yet if you are in the Brotherhood, it is more likely that you are born in the Brotherhood, and this is your entire life. And it is the same with the Elite.

As a reference, the presidents are somewhere in the Middle Brotherhood. The Rockefellers are at the top of the Brotherhood, while the Rothschilds are in the Elite. And if you know nothing about all these, and mostly if you have a low or medium income and you are preoccupied mostly with tempered addictions, entertainment, family and social problems, and shortages of all kind, while tending and providing to your family throughout life, then you are from the Masses.

What exactly is there to know, and more importantly, what are these tricks and shenanigans? Is this similar to exploiting financial markets throughout consensual bust – boom cycles? No, not at all, since as stated above, the Consensual Matrix expands to cover a great part of the wider world and it is eternal, while always using the same tricks and shenanigans to make it possible in the wider world and keep it instated. And since the Consensual Matrix spreads here to cover you, now it is very easy for you to see and understand the Consensual Matrix firsthand, since it is you feeding it in every manner throughout life. While it is also you evading all laws, in order to be allowed to do so.

Yet the Consensual Matrix does not engulf the entire world despite of what anyone may claim, since the Consensual Matrix engulfs you only when you live your life on lower developmental levels. Because when you live your life at the intelligent human level, you stand above beliefs, hierarchies, jurisdictions, and entire ideologies, you are capable to reason and therefore distinguish the good from the bad yourself, you choose your own, natural behavior and lifestyle, you fulfill your own, natural meaning in life and in this world, and therefore the Consensual Matrix cannot reach you.

But how can the Consensual Matrix reach you? How can it engulf this world despite of all laws set in place to protect your rights? How is everything done? Very simple. There is an entire new, consensual environment created where you live, and you may choose to live your life consensually if you please, because you are allowed to do so. This is the Consensual Matrix, it is consensual, and when you choose to live your life in it, you exit your natural, genuine, real, objective human environment, which is this entire world. You state clearly that it is your choice to become consensual and you sign all the necessary forms, and since all higher laws and all human rights protecting you come straight from Life and the Divine and they address only the natural, objective world, now when you stay in the Consensual Matrix to serve the Consensual Matrix, you wave them implicitly. This is how anyone may exploit you and harvest you in every manner, and this is exactly how everything is done. This sounds as a cheap scenario, but everything has been going on since ever, you do so and you force your children to do so, along with their children. While the natural laws are clear, since for each world, reality, and environment, being natural, artificial, or consensual, you have one identity, one body, one self, and one meaning to fulfill, and one jurisdiction to abide to. And the Consensual Matrix has all requirements defined, as it remains distinct from the real world, while the higher laws cannot enter its jurisdictions.

Yet you have always been living in this world, breathing air, eating food and drinking water, a real living world filled by life and created by the Divine, so how can this be now the Consensual Matrix? The Consensual Matrix is consensual and not real, it is fiat, and it parallels in this manner the real world. And if the Consensual Matrix states so, then it must be true, just because the Consensual Matrix always writes its own laws and regulations meant to prove itself right, in a major conflict of interest, and it works. Everything is consensual and nothing else, but it really works. And you know it, because you have been fulfilling consensual meanings your entire life by using money and taking orders. Your human rights have always been infringed, while all authorities do not actually follow Life and the Divine, but the Consensual Matrix.

Yet all these are empiric observations, and you have to have accurate facts in order to see the Consensual Matrix and understand it in an intelligent manner. The Consensual Matrix is consensual and therefore it cannot be seen or touched, yet the Consensual Matrix is everywhere, and therefore you cannot miss its presence. And since the Consensual Matrix engulfs you many times since birth, as it does so in a legal manner, in order not to infringe all laws and rights, it is through documents and legal statements, procedures, and signatures that you may see it now. Even more, the entire bureaucracy relates to the Consensual Matrix, because the higher laws coming from the Divine have one statement: you have the right to fulfill your needs and meanings wherever you are.

And now, let us see this trick making the entire matrix possible. You never live your life in the genuine, natural human environment as you may expect, which is this entire world, the intelligent human environment allowing you to fulfill your genuine, natural human meaning, as love and the Divine, but you live in a consensual environment instead, since birth. It is a consensual environment, and I refer to it as the Consensual Matrix. The Consensual Matrix is abstract, but not optional, and not holographic as you may assume. And you may see it right away, since you have an entire consensual corporation that you use in order to interact within the Consensual Matrix, because the higher and lower laws do not allow you to do so as a genuine, living human being. And this consensual corporation is a genuine, accurate, existing corporation that has your name, but written in uppercase letters. This is not your name, this is not your identity, and this is not you. If you do not believe it, just search through your purse and wallet for your documents, to find them having this name written in uppercase letters, which is not your name as a living human being, but it is your brand or trademark as a corporation.

And this is what you are as a corporation in the consensual matrix. While you are the living human being in the real world, as you have these two environments to choose. The real world where you are a living human being, or the multitude of jurisdictions of the Consensual Matrix where you are a consensual corporation if you carry your documents with you, and if you claim directly or implicitly to be a corporation.

And in general, if you are from the Masses, you lack awareness of any of these, and you fall in the Consensual Matrix continuously. If you are from the Brotherhood, you know all these, and you still have to remain in the Consensual Matrix when you are ordered. But when you are off duty, you may choose to remain in the real world, if you are allowed. As when the police stops you, and you inform them in various manners that you are the living human being in the real world. So they have to let you go, for you to tend to your normal life as a living human being. Because the police is a corporation, and cannot have you in any jurisdiction as a living human being, since all jurisdictions are meant for corporations.

Additionally, all corporations and all jurisdictions operate here on Earth in order to serve minutely the living human beings. And therefore, as a living human being, you can order around all corporations from all jurisdictions, and they have to serve you in every manner that you desire as a living human being. Yet do not push your luck, since the Brotherhood takes you out whoever or whatever you are.

And in general, you are a corporation and not a living human being in the current consensual society, despite of what all politicians and public workers may state. And this is why you have an accurate bureaucracy throughout this world, but when it comes to life and living human beings, you always have shortages, poverty, misery, mistakes, calamities, and errors, affecting your real life, but never affecting the Consensual Matrix. Because the Consensual Matrix is flawless.

How much is you, the genuine living human being, and how much is your corporation in this world and throughout life? The answer to this question is relevant in identifying your true meanings in life, consensual and natural, as a consensual corporation or as a genuine living human being. You may find this answer right away, just by studying these same documents, everything that you have, as ID cards, licenses, permits, certificates, policies, diplomas, accounts, achievements, and receipts. And wherever you find your name written in uppercase letters, that is not you, but your corporation. While those specific documents state precisely that everything there is done on behalf of that corporation. Whenever you find with your name written normally in lowercase letters, that specific part of your life belongs to you, the genuine living human being.

And this is not the case only with people corporations, but with business corporations, city corporations, nation corporations, political corporations, and financial corporations. In general, wherever you find names written in uppercase letters, that is a corporation, it is consensual in nature, yet it is still a consensual body or being. And therefore, it exists through laws, oaths, statements, consensus, and legal agreements. These are your oaths and agreements, and since you are a genuine living human being, these agreements and consensuses making all corporations possible are respected by all laws, since the higher laws respect all your choices throughout life.

And now, through the same agreements and consensuses, all corporations may be sold, bought, owned, and exploited in every manner, not necessarily by you, but by whoever took possession of them from you. While it is clearly stated on these documents and on the documents that the current owners of your corporation possess, along with your family corporation and your children's corporations, since the rich and the powerful own these. In general, if you have the certificate, then you still have a chance to have ownership of that item, trademark, or corporation, which is the case with your car. This sounds trivial, yet there are entire nations where citizens have never seen their Certificate of Birth, since others hold these, their actual owners. The word 'citizen' itself defines corporations and not genuine living beings, along with words as 'person,' 'persons,' and 'body,' and probably even the words 'human,' and 'recipient.' Because as you are, you have slight chances that you actually own your own corporation along with its debt and achievements, and along with your family corporation, despite of what you are told and promised.

And now, this topic of the human meaning becomes significantly more complex. Because while you might be more interested in fulfilling your intelligent human meaning as a living human being, all your authorities and those owning and controlling these authorities are interested in your consensual meanings in this world and throughout life, implementing these consensual meanings now through countless of ideologies, districts, and jurisdictions spanning the Consensual Matrix, to make you in this manner work and live your entire life for them. Serving them continuously. This enters in conflict with your natural meaning in life and in this world, you certainly feel it throughout life and it makes you unfulfilled, and this kills you in the end, whenever you become worthless for the Consensual Matrix.

How can you exit the Consensual Matrix? Nobody wants to exit the Consensual Matrix, but only to enter it if they happen to be out, and then to advance high up its hierarchies of power, profiting and exploiting alongside as much as possible. Because the Consensual Matrix cannot have you if you happen to admit that you are a living human being, since you live in the real, natural, objective environment as a living human being, you fulfill your intelligent human meaning in life and in this world, you have your human rights, while you are protected by the higher laws and by any higher being protecting these laws. Even more, since all jurisdictions in this world are in the Consensual Matrix, there are no jurisdictions, courts, and no laws and regulations restricting your natural living human meaning, behavior, lifestyle, and rights in the real, natural living world. However, the Consensual Matrix will always attempt to force you or trick you to admit that you are always in the Consensual Matrix, therefore under their jurisdiction, and therefore under its control and command.

While now it is only a matter of how aware you are of all these, and of how you use your words throughout your statements, because your slightest mistake gives the Consensual

Matrix the chance to take you back. And when it does, it destroys you as quickly and as dreadfully as it can, all being done legally. Never underestimate the Consensual Matrix, since it spans most of the wider world, it is as powerful as the wider world, and no one and nothing can ever affect it.

You represent your corporation in this manner since birth, through it you live in the Consensual Matrix in this manner since birth, around money, hierarchies, power, bureaucracy, influence, and material pleasure, every moment of your intelligent human life. You live your life in this manner as a consensual corporation, and you share the consensual meaning of your corporation, which is to gain more money, more power, more influence, more dominance, more wealth, and more authority, at all costs, even at the expense of failing fulfilling your genuine natural meaning in life, which always remains related to love and to the Divine. I study this subject in details throughout a multitude of books in this series, since it is highly significant in understanding you, this world, and your place, meaning, and condition in life and in this world.

But are you actually a traitor in life and in this world by seeking and fulfilling meanings that have nothing to do with love and the Divine? Yes, certainly, since society, along with its multitude of ideologies, states this clearly and continuously. Because all ideologies claim that they are good, extraordinary, on your side, and on your behalf. Yet through them, you end up seeking other things in life besides love and the Divine, and everyone does so. And this is the case just because your own needs demand it, mostly your consensual needs, while your needs are countless. And to add to them, your need for money and more money can overpass by far your entire natural meaning in life, while society can easily achieve this through crisis, shortages, and austerity measures. And this is exactly why at the beginning of this book you had the feeling that meanings cannot be only about love and the Divine, because existence is more complex today in this world. And it is more to understand here, since this is only the surface, and you never find it in bestseller books and movies.

Yet this might never be your case, mostly if you achieve to live your life at the third developmental level, which is the intelligent human level. Yet there are not too many people living life at the third developmental level, or none at all. Just look around now, to find how all meanings in this world relate to money, material achievements, pleasure, power, lies, servitude, drugs, vices, and influence.

But these are bad or lost people you may say, since they think in this material manner, or this is what ideologies state. While they make you assume that luckily, you manage it better this life, by keeping your life straight, while seeking only love and the Divine throughout life. Are they right? No, since everybody is equal in everything throughout life. There are no good and bad people in this world despite of what society and authorities claim, and even more, everybody has the same meaning in life and in this world, and it is good, if it is genuinely human. While as we see throughout this book, it always relates to love and to the Divine. This world is never divided into the good and the bad as ideologies state, or into the superior and the inferior, or into the lost and the found, because these are only tricks used to divide and conquer people. While this world is just the same. But ideologies use these simplistic beliefs in order to control you and the entire world, by assuring everybody that they are the chosen ones. While promising you everything, and this is how they have what they want.

And there is social pressure, forcing you to follow ideologies, otherwise you become the bad and the unwanted in this world. You may see it well happening everywhere, since this simple trick of good versus evil took over the media and entertainment, to expand now into justice, politics, military, and even in education.

But can you see it well in your case too? Because it might interfere now while understanding your actual meaning, natural and consensual. You could see it well if you could only be able to reason independently, free of the multitude of beliefs coming from all ideologies. And you cannot even assume that you are free of all these, since you are born with them. And this is how most are still at the core of your cognitive system, altering your reasoning to make you now accept them as accurate facts and as natural laws, impairing you now to distinguish the good from the bad yourself.

Then how exactly can you tell the good from the bad on your own? Currently, you have your ideology helping you understand your own meaning in life and in this world. And depending on where you live, this ideology may be social, religious, scientific, financial, political, and national. And many times, this stands as your only source defining your meaning in life and in this world, in a conflict of interest. Even more, whenever others tell you that there is more out there in life and in this world besides what your ideology claims, you are ready to challenge them in any manner, only to remain assured that your ideology is all that there can be, defining right now on its own the good from the bad for you, along with your entire meaning in life and in this world. And all ideologies, hierarchies, and jurisdictions stand at the first level, offering you only a first level meaning in life and in this world. While you are a living human being by nature, and should have an intelligent human meaning in life and in this world, at the third level.

As a reference, just study your favorite encyclopedia if you are allowed, to find out what the multitude of religions, schools of thought, and social, political, and national ideologies have to claim about your own meaning in life and in this world, about the meaning of humanity in life and in this world, or about the meaning of life in this world. And the diversity of meanings that you will find there will surprise you. While life is only one, and it should have one meaning, similar everywhere, since people are very similar everywhere and they behave similarly.

How can anyone have a different meaning according to each one of these ideologies? Are they true? And why do you have the feeling that there is more to your life and to this world than what these ideologies state? Yet if your ideology happens to fulfill you entirely, then you might have already achieved your meaning in life and in this world, and therefore nothing that you encounter and learn from now on holds more meaning than what you already have, than what your ideology already states, than what is already provided to you.

Yet can there be anything else out there worth mentioning here besides what your ideology states? No, nothing at all, and this is always the case when you consider ideological meanings in this world, since these are of the first cognitive level, and therefore you are always meant to accept them exactly as they come, wholly and unchanged. And when you identify your meaning in life and in this world at this first consensual ideological level, then everything defining and characterizing you stands at the first consensual level, including your thinking, development, abilities, awareness, lifestyle, responsibility, achievements, rights, identity, status, strength, and connectivity. Servitude itself is a first level consensual behavior, and it is not possible without an ideological meaning in life to hold its first level pattern, otherwise you break free and walk away.

And this is why, now, when you look back throughout history, you find this world drenched in blood, misery, darkness, slavery, and loss, because this is exactly what the beliefs and meanings of the first developmental level do. Because ideologies charm you with extraordinary meanings in life that you must always achieve, and with extraordinary rewards afterwards if you ever achieve these meanings. And then, whenever you look back in life and in this world, to see what you truly did, and this is what you find. Because you are never as extraordinary and as superior as ideologies promise, and this is the case just because humans are equal in abilities, achievements, and fulfillment, they are equal in rights, and therefore they are worthy of a similar development, an intelligent human development, despite of anything that hundreds of thousands of ideologies currently state throughout this world.

Does this mean that your specific ideology is wrong, and your meaning in life is not exactly to find love and to serve the

Divine as it always states? If your specific ideology implements love and good behavior throughout life, while it never summons you to do anything bad or negative, then you may consider yourself lucky. However, how can you ever distinguish the good from the bad yourself, in order to be able to assess your own ideology, when you are forced to think through the same beliefs that your own ideology implements, in a conflict of interest? Besides, many ideologies forbid you entirely to judge and assess them in any manner, while they even forbid you to use your reasoning altogether, allowing you only to think and see this world through their specific beliefs. And this is how you always remain in a loop of reasoning while judging ideologies, obtaining positive answers by default. While this little detail is enough to render this world tightly controlled.

Does this mean that this world is doomed to remain under the same totalitarian regimes and false ideologies? No, not at all, and this is the case not because these are not strong enough to control this world, since they truly are, but this is the case because ideologies of all kind, good and bad, implement consensual beliefs and therefore consensual meanings in life and in this world, contradicting in this manner your own intrinsic, genuine, natural meanings in life and in this world. And it never matters how capable ideologies are, because they can never match Life herself and the Divine, since Life and the Divine are the ones sending you your natural needs and feelings through your cognitive system, including love, your true, natural love. So yes, love and the Divine are your true meaning in life and in this world, if you can only make sure that you follow them on your own, continuously throughout life, and not through rituals and ideologies. Make sure that you follow love, Life, and the Divine through everything that you do and achieve in life naturally, through your own human nature, reasoning, moral, and virtue, through your own natural, intelligent human needs, through your own freedom, and through your own natural, genuine feelings, including love.

What exactly are ideologies and what are they doing in this

world? What is their exact meaning in life and in this world? Ideologies are sets of beliefs stated by people or by higher beings meant to make life and the entire world better or worse, or meant to free people or to render them under control, since there are good and bad ideologies in principle, addressing the good and the bad to everyone alike.

Yet ideologies always remain as finite sets of statements and beliefs that fit well into a book or two, and this renders ideologies useless on a longer term, their sheer simplicity and triviality compared to Life and to the Divine. While Life, this world, the Divine, and your intelligent human needs are endless, very capable, and highly consistent among themselves.

And now, as you look back throughout history, you may see ideologies as temporary consensual social patches ruling this world from one regime to another and from one revolution to another. While it is only through their number and manipulation that ideologies are capable to rule this world together, one after another, one set of consensual beliefs after another, and therefore one consensual meaning in life after another. Yet as stated above, ideologies are good and bad in principle, and it is enough to look back throughout history to see what they did to this world in one age or another, in order for you to be able to tell what they are doing to this world now, and therefore to tell them apart in this manner.

And history goes on, and many times, it repeats itself. For how long? Endlessly, because ideologies are very capable in altering your own intelligent human meaning in life and in this world, rendering you in this manner incapable to distinguish the good from the bad on your own. Or this is the case if you live your life on lower developmental levels, at the zero addicted level, first consensual servitude ideological level, and second animal intuitive level. Because from the third intelligent human developmental level up, you are capable through your intelligent human reasoning, meaning, and awareness to distinguish on your own the good from the bad, the relevant from the irrelevant, and the useful from the harmful. Or you may do so if you only know how to identify and bypass your beliefs. Because at the intelligent human level and higher, you are capable to distinguish on your own between beliefs and genuine knowledge, and this is the case just because genuinely developed humans are capable to use their powerful human reasoning throughout life. Or this is the case when humans are free to reason, since totalitarian regimes and ideologies forbid independent reasoning to humans, along with the rest of the human cognitive abilities.

Is your ideology good or bad? You always consider it good, just because you use its own beliefs in order to assess it. And this is how you always obtain reassuring results, because all ideologies make sure to implement excellent beliefs about themselves.

If your specific ideology is truly good or bad it may depend, since as stated above, ideologies count in hundreds of thousands, and they fight for identity and supremacy, at the expense of your own identity, natural development, lifelong achievements, and genuine meaning in life and in this world. Just look around to find this to be the case. Because your meaning in life and in this world is mostly good, but it may also be dreadful to others and even to you and your loved ones, and this is always the case while following ideologies. Since this is not exactly your own natural, genuine meaning in life and in this world, but your consensual, induced one. Because your meaning may be of many types, natures, classes, and developmental levels, as we have already seen, while it is significant to identify yours.

And if your meaning is consensual, at the first ideological, juridical, hierarchical, or stereotypical level, then it is hijacked to be in this manner, mostly from birth. And if this is the case with you, then your chance to regain your own natural, intelligent human meaning in life and in this world is very slim. If you even have the desire to regain it anymore, since ideologies turn your cognitive system upside down, they change the good into bad and the bad into good, they change the natural into consensual and the consensual into natural, and if you had ever wondered why all those people in the news behave in such an outrageous manner, there is an ideology there doing all the work, making them believe that they are good and worthy the entire time. And do not expect that other ideologies are better just because they are not in the news, because the media is biased.

And now, when you move your perspective even higher, you may see the large groups of people and even entire nations controlled minutely by distinct, opposing ideologies, to the point where they are capable to smash these opposing groups of people one against another, destroying everything and everyone in this manner. And this is a form of genocide, one among many. And for everybody involved in these opposing ideologies, conflicts, and acts of terror, their sole meaning in life is to create the big smash capable to hurt everybody, even the entire world.

Is your ideology still neutral and relatively safe? Just study the news closely, all news, from both sides. Because it is not necessarily your ideology harming you and through you harming this world, but those controlling your ideology do the entire harm, through your ideology, and therefore through you.

Or is it you doing the harm? Because you can never distinguish who or what to blame. Because if you still attempt to blame those controlling ideologies and through them controlling this world, know that these people up on top of society do nothing, or this is what they claim, in order not to be blamed. While they wait patiently for the entire world to turn nicely in their favor, always having the same meaning for this world, supreme ownership and domination of this world, with your kind gone, exterminated, and out of the way, whoever you are and whatever you are promised, if you are not one of them and part of their genetic line.

Yet this is the case only if you happen to live your life at the first developmental level, which is the servitude and dogmatic level. Because ideologies can never reach you on higher developmental levels, not at their bottom among the suffering, not in the middle among hierarchies, and not at the top among profiteers. And this is the case just because at higher developmental levels, you know exactly how to find your way out of dogma and ideologies, just by following your intelligent human needs.

What exactly are the human needs? I study needs of all classes and levels throughout several books of this series. There are many genuine, natural human needs, all at the third intelligent level, and they are highly complex. And many times, they are highly abstract and therefore highly difficult to identify and fulfill. While you can never develop to your intelligent human level, if you do not fulfill them, or you remain at the animal level, which is the second developmental level, or at the servitude level, which is the first developmental level, or even at the disabled, addiction level, which is the zero level.

Yet science and education will never explain the intelligent human needs to you, so you never know them. And this is how you end up living your life on lower developmental levels. You may find many of the human needs stated throughout encyclopedias and even throughout ideologies not as human needs, but stated as genuine meanings in life. While needs are never meanings, but needs only stand at the base of all meanings, forming, comprising, and defining meanings in this manner one fulfillment at a time.

And if you are successful throughout the fulfillment of all needs, going in this manner through your entire development, only then you may have the chance to fulfill your human meaning in life and in this world, your intelligent human meaning. Yet the intelligent human meanings are more than developmental in nature, since only one human need among all is developmental in nature, and a very important one. In the following chapter, we study needs, meanings, and the rest of relevant concepts in all details and from all perspectives, mostly from cognitive perspectives. Yet in general, while you tend to fulfill your needs mostly for yourself, meanings are needs that you fulfill for everybody else, many times for the entire world.

How developed are you exactly? You are developed at higher levels just because you are willing to read this book and because you are capable to understand it. And this chapter is mostly empiric, and easy to understand. Because if you happen to lack either your determination or understanding of the third cognitive level, necessary to match the nature of this book, then you feel boredom, discomfort, or even exasperation, which are punishments associated with important lower level needs, which try to make you do something else instead. And this is how your cognitive system, if it is at a lower developmental level, tries to get you engaged in the fulfillment of needs of a lower level, as fulfilling your physiological needs from the second level, as eating and reproducing, or making more money or gaining more power and influence if you happen to live your life at the first consensual level, or taking more drugs if you happen to live your life at the zero addicted level.

Yet these lower developmental levels are not your case, or at least not right now, since you are more developed just by reading this book, just by being able to understand this book, just by being interested in this book and not only in the lower level activities mentioned above. And you know it because you feel it, you have it in you, just by being rewarded plentifully with extraordinary feelings only to keep you reading this book. And you can certainly tell the difference, while you also know that if you are not reading this book right now, which is, if you are not maintaining yourself at the third, human developmental level, then you fall again at the lower developmental levels mentioned above, at any of them, since society provides them plentifully today. While life is less consistent on lower developmental levels, cheap and consensual, below your expectations, and so you learn to stay away from them. Because your own natural human meaning is embedded intrinsically in your cognitive system, and you already feel it and know what you have to do through your complex system of needs and feelings. And if you do not manage to remain on top of your meanings, then you never reach your intelligent human achievements, and you never develop to your true potential. And Life punishes you then, through your entire cognitive system, through dreadful feelings, continuously throughout life, when you remain at lower developmental levels. And it is so terrible, that it pushes you to drugs and medication and even to cruelty and despair, and you might have already been there, since this is what everybody receives throughout life when they fail their intelligent human meaning.

And our question persists, what are meanings exactly, if they are not those stated by regimes, politicians, and entire ideologies and jurisdictions? And even more, what are these intelligent human meanings? As a reference, you fulfill all your needs for yourself and for your loved ones, in a rather selfish manner. While you fulfill your meanings for everybody and everything else, for no direct, material compensation, but only because you feel it and because you want it, which is the case at the third intelligent human level.

More importantly, you are fulfilled when you fulfill your meanings, since you are rewarded intrinsically with very good feelings to do so. Yet there is more than receiving good feelings when you fulfill your meanings at the intelligent human level, because you do so through your reasoning just as well, in order to do good deeds in this world, to help this world, to make this world a better, loving, equal, prosperous place.

For example, you might feel your meanings as a care in this world. Yet if you are in the current consensual Brotherhood, you might even get in trouble for the fulfillment of your intelligent human meanings, and then you have to burn your care, as it is called. Because you cannot live your life at the first consensual level and at the third intelligent human level simultaneously.

And this knowledge was supposed to be trivial. In other words, while you use sources and resources from your environment in order to fulfill your needs, you become a source for others to fulfill their needs, and even an entire environment, through the fulfillment of your own meanings, helping others fulfill their needs. Since the others come to fulfill their needs through you, through meanings.

Good, meaningful, important books become available through the fulfillment of someone's meaning in this world, the author behind these books. Since he spends decades of tedious work fulfilling his meanings, for you to fulfill your intelligent human needs now, through all his books. It is the same with genuine art, relevant technology, good teachers, and genuine doctors and healers, since these people work hard for the fulfillment of the needs of others, and they do so through the fulfillment of their own meanings, always being rewarded intrinsically just as well.

Since as you notice, there is not much difference between needs and meanings from your own perspective, as they are rewarded intrinsically through similar good feelings even by the same intelligences. But it is a tremendous difference for the rest of this world, since many are capable now to fulfill their needs through your own meanings in life and in this world.

And this is why it is important to consider the concept of meaning, yet as you notice, when you research it in the current society, you find diverting facts, as beliefs, utopias, and entire ideologies. Even more, all the intelligent human meanings in this world do not come separately, distinctly, or individually, but they manifest as an entire environment, the intelligent human environment. The intelligent human environment is similar to the family that you have at home, only that the intelligent human environment spans this world, comprising everything that you need to fulfill your needs and meanings at the intelligent human level, to develop to your intelligent human level, and to live your life at the intelligent human level, in continuous intelligent human fulfillment. Only in this manner, you can fulfill Life and the Divine, since you are an intelligent human living being by nature, and this is why they have brought here in this world an intelligent human being, and not anything else.

Yet today it is different, since the current human society is consensual, at the first servitude level on purpose, demanding that you erase the intelligent human environment and that you maintain the current Consensual Matrix instated through all your ideologies, beliefs, stereotypes, and entire jurisdictions, and this is what you do. Because it is never a matter of choice, what developmental level you should adopt, or what meaning you should fulfill today, but it is a matter of constraint, development, and choice. While you cannot exactly blame it on constraint, ignorance, and underdevelopment either, since this world is full of trolls, and these cannot wait to harm you and your loved ones in every manner. Ask the higher selves, since this is what they like. And now, since they have the chance, this is what they do.

Yet not everybody is a troll harming humanity, just as not everybody is in the Elite, exploiting and exterminating humanity, just as not everybody is a servant in the current hierarchic Brotherhood, erasing the intelligent human environment, just as not everybody is in the Masses, taking drugs and obeying everything blindly while harming this world.

But is there anyone living life at the intelligent human level, in the intelligent human environment, fulfilling intelligent human meanings in this world, and actually helping this world? No. Do you actually see these genuinely developed people anywhere? No. Is this entire idea of meanings a utopia? No, since the intrinsic needs and feelings are there for you to fulfill your meanings continuously in order to tend to the entire human world, only that you never do, remaining unfulfilled. And so you take drugs instead, decaying.

Why don't you ever fulfill your intelligent human needs and meanings? Through ignorance and even enforcement if you are from the Masses, or through servitude and enforcement if you are from the current hierarchic Brotherhood, or through underdevelopment if you are from the Elite. Since this does not happen only on Earth, but throughout the entire Consensual Matrix, which spans most of the wider world.

Because you are not allowed, directly or implicitly, to develop at the intelligent human level, to fulfill your intelligent human needs and meanings, and through these, to form the intelligent human environment necessary for everybody else to fulfill their intelligent human needs and meanings and to remain developed at the intelligent human level. Since this is the existential circle making everything possible, currently broken on purpose, for various reasons. And this is why you are not able to fulfill your natural human needs today, since you do not have the means to do so, because society never helps, and many times, it never allows the fulfillment of higher level needs and meanings.

Yet you persist fulfilling your human needs most of the time, standing above doctrine and ideologies, just because you seek to read this kind of books, and therefore because you already seek to develop at your intelligent human level. You seek in this manner to follow your natural, higher meaning in life and in this world, and this is the third intelligent developmental level, not the first consensual one.

What exactly is your meaning in life and in this world? As stated above, if you are interested in this kind of books, then you are currently undergoing your genuine, natural human development, fulfilling intelligent human needs, as the need for true, genuine, important human knowledge, and even higher knowledge, beyond the third intelligent level. There is coherence between needs, meanings, and destiny in life and in this world as we see throughout the book, and if you can only identify these, then you have the chance to remain within your own natural, intelligent human behavior, reasoning, environment, lifestyle, and therefore meaning and development.

Yet people will read books only to prove that their own beliefs and ideologies remain superior in life and in this world. There are also people who are ordered to read books in order to write reports and label them accordingly, labels defining now their accessibility to the public. And this is exactly how you find books of irrelevant importance as best sellers in this world, this is what the public reads, this is what the public learns, and this is how the public behaves. It is called indoctrination. Since this is exactly how you erase the intelligent human environment, as ordered. And consequently, these are the world and the environment that humans create.

As you may see it everywhere, in its full spectacle, since it is the current first level consensual, servitude, indoctrinated, ideological, hierarchical society. Because your meaning in life and in this world, exactly as you identify and implement it through your own reasoning and behavior, is the one creating your world now, along with the world of everybody else. And consequently, your meaning is exactly what you now get to enjoy for good and for worse, alongside your loved ones and alongside the entire world. Because meanings become integral part of behaviors, they do so through all needs, these needs define permanently all achievements and failures, along with all changes in this world, and these changes construct entire lines of causality along with entire lifelines and timelines here in this world and everywhere else in the wider world. Because everything is connected in this manner, everything is part of the One, and you must identify everything before you attempt studying such a complex topic as meaning, any meaning, including your own human meaning in life and in this world, your intelligent human meaning.

What irrelevant bestseller books am I considering above? Bestseller books are not the only ones bringing irrelevant learning material to the public, since science remains entirely irrelevant in this topic, at least the current science, along with education, and along with entertainment and media in general. As you know it well, because currently, alternative media along with alternative science and alternative education are capable to fulfill your needs for genuine learning and genuine development more than their mainstream counterparts. And it always relates with ideologies and meanings in life and in this world, and with the specific sets of beliefs that those controlling society carry, since they end up controlling this world according to these. In other words, those controlling society and this world do so while passing to this world and therefore to you the exact first level consensual meanings that they happen to carry themselves. And this is how an entire world wonders now if the Earth is actually flat, just because those controlling society have not changed their belief that the

Earth is flat for millennia.

And this is why you may find only motivational books considering meanings in life and in this world today, along with religious, philosophical, and spiritual books, but no scientific books, all based on beliefs but not on genuine facts, all rendering you not smarter, but only indoctrinated. Which is perfect if indoctrination is what you seek in life, just because as stated above, meanings in life can come at all developmental levels, including the first level, which is the consensual, servitude, ideological, juridical, indoctrination level.

And today, all meanings tend to be of the first consensual level, just look around to see them for yourself. While this entire movement that this world undergoes today very slowly toward learning, understanding, righteousness, wellbeing, compassion, and mostly freedom, is based on third level needs, third level abilities, and therefore third level meanings, the intelligent human meanings.

Because there is a difference between genuine accurate knowledge and beliefs, since through beliefs, you can never reason, but you may only think in slogans and in numbered phrases, throughout endless monologues or debates. While genuine reasoning characterizes genuinely developed humans the most, reasoning always based on accurate facts and on intelligent research. And this is exactly what you cannot find in bestseller books today, genuine knowledge and intelligent reasoning, but you find only beautiful, motivational words, along with beautiful slogans and beautiful thoughts. And when you repeat these long enough, they can certainly indoctrinate you. While your intelligent human meaning in life and in this world might not be exactly about slogans, motivation, and indoctrination, but about countless of natural, connected occurrences, taking places throughout countless of circumstances, all forming your diverse experience, causing your continuous development. This is part of your natural meaning in life and in this world, and nothing that a handful of people from the top of this world can ever do to match it, since your genuine, natural human meaning relates to Life and to the Divine, while their consensual conspiracies and ideologies have meanings against Life and against the Divine. Because you have either Life and the Divine, or you have the Consensual Matrix, since you cannot have them both.

And this always happens, while no one seems to care, because many ideologies simply alter or even reverse the concepts that give meaning to your life and to this world. And in this manner, powerful higher beings are invited to replace the Divine and to rule this world as they please, and people believe in them, and do as are told.

Could it happen that the Divine has a specific meaning, just for you, to serve in a specific manner, and now this is exactly what you must do until you die, if you can only find out what it is? Everything depends on whom you are referring here. Is it the true Divine that you are considering, or only various impostors claiming to be the Divine, as these tend to do? Because you always have to serve these impostors many times in a humanly manner, through physical servitude and even through sexual work. Since this is exactly where the words 'venerate' and 'venerable' come from. Because the true Divine is all that exists everywhere and in all realities, including all these realities, including you and your life, your behavior, society and this entire world, along with all worlds above. And therefore, you are already serving the Divine continuously throughout life, through your comprehensive natural intelligent human behavior, through your intelligent human meanings, and through every moment of your life. Or this is the case when you manage to fulfill your genuine, natural meaning in life, through the cumulative fulfillment of all natural human needs and meanings that you receive, identify, and fulfill successfully. Because through the needs that you miss or that you fulfill partially or that you do not fulfill at all, you end up failing Life and the Divine. And you certainly feel it, because they punish you dreadfully, through all the bad feelings that you receive throughout life. Life herself is a supreme correspondence of the Supreme Being, and therefore Life and the Divine are the same, when you perceive them from the same living perspective. Since the Divine is alive, and Life is his life. Or Mother Earth, or Mother Nature, as she is commonly called. While Intelligence is his intelligence, or the Universal Mind, as it is commonly called. And while Interconnectivity is the One, his Oneness. While this is omnipresence, omniscience, and omnipotence.

And the more successful you are at fulfilling your needs, all your natural needs, of higher and lower levels, the more you serve Life and the Divine. Even more, by serving others, including random higher powerful beings, along with masters and authorities here on Earth, directly or throughout hierarchies, it takes away from your time and effort that you should invest in fulfilling your own genuine, natural needs. And this is how you fail your own natural, genuine meaning in life, which is to serve the true Divine. And even more, throughout your servitude, you are ordered to interfere negatively with the natural meanings of those around. And this is how you end up erasing the intelligent human environment, making the fulfillment of all needs impossible, while harming this world. And many times, you fall into servitude unknowingly, even just by reading the specific lower level bestseller books mentioned above.

And now, with all relevant intelligent human material erased and absent, they are the only books that you may find to read, or the only movies to watch, the only news, the only documentaries, the only music to listen to. Because they are full of the same kind of slogans, motivation, and indoctrination that take you away from the fulfillment of your natural meaning in life, ending up fulfilling instead these consensual meanings, which should never apply to you as a living human being.

What is wrong with slogans, motivation, and indoctrination? It might seem inaccurate now, but these three are capable to determine you to engage in any behavior that they choose, even in a consensual behavior, rendering you willing to alter your genuine meaning in life and in this world in any consensual manner. Just study now in details all current motivational books from any library, to find them applying only a patch or bandage to your mood, willingness, thinking, and behavior, just because these mainstream books are not capable to explain to you your entire meaning in life and in this world as they claim. And therefore, they are not capable to help you think and act in the most adequate manner in society, in this world, and throughout life, according to your own natural human meanings.

And it is not a matter of principle, of virtue, or of being correct in life and this world to deliver to Life and to the Divine everything that these expect from you in the exact manner that they do, but Life and the Divine will never leave you alone until you serve them, until you do everything that you casually do. And they punish you by sending you pain and discomfort through your cognitive system, and they punish you severely in this manner until you fulfill your natural needs as they deserve. And if you persist to ignore, neglect, or temper with your natural needs and with their fulfillment in any manner, then Life and the Divine will do everything only for you to get back to your senses and do exactly as you are supposed to do, fulfill your own natural needs, fulfill your intelligent human meanings, and nothing else.

Do Life and the Divine know that there are already hundreds of thousands of ideologies that have long altered all natural meanings in every manner, distancing the people from Life and from the Divine? No, not at all, because Life and the Divine are known to discard entire worlds and civilizations for failing even slightly, and they will do the same to Earth very soon, since they always expect the best from the people of Earth.

And then, when you manage to do and be the best, when you manage to fulfill your natural meaning through everything that you are and do, then it is the other way around, because Life and the Divine reward you plentifully with love and happiness, and you feel fulfilled. This is what you want throughout life and nothing else, and you are ready to do everything only to keep it coming. Because your meaning in life is love and the Divine, and nothing else, if you are only capable to understand the Divine and your love, and how it comes and for what reason, since this is how you understand your genuine meaning in life and in this world.

But when you neglect your natural needs and your natural meaning for any consensual reason, or when you are naturally incapable to fulfill your meaning in life and in this world, then Life and the Divine will take you out and dispose of you at once, making room in this manner for someone else to come and take your place in life and in this world to fulfill your meaning, which now becomes theirs. When there is no one else to do the job and fulfill your meaning in life and in this world, this is when all problems start, since Life and the Divine are ready to dispose of entire species, entire societies, entire civilizations, and entire worlds only to have things done right for them, if only one desired outcome or meaning is compromised, for any reason, and under any circumstance.

And this is exactly why ideologies instate themselves only temporarily, before they fall, because entire masses of people have to fall before ideologies fall. Yet other ideologies come to take their place, since they are connected, and many times, they are controlled by the same higher people or higher beings profiting the entire time. While I refer to this entire consensual ideological connectivity as the Consensual Matrix, and I study it in details throughout many books of this series.

And this is why the great majority of people in this world have to live their lives intoxicated or on medication today, throughout hospitals, jails, and mental institutions, or in concealment and hypocrisy behind masks, just because their own intelligent human meaning in life cannot correspond to the specific consensual meaning that society and all authorities controlling society determine, define, and demand from people today. While their mind and feelings will never leave them alone until they fulfill their natural, genuine needs, driving them mad in this manner, and forcing them to addictions.

And if you happen to remain unaware that there are consensual meanings in life and in this world, currently displacing your intelligent human meaning, while you happen to drink and smoke for no reason at all, or if you ignore that meanings in life can be consensual, and that they can be hijacked for various agendas, or even that your life and behavior have a meaning and that everything that you do, achieve, and experience throughout life also has a meaning, then you might be interested in learning more about the meaning of your human meaning, since meanings are very complex.

We should consider soon the most common meanings of life, in the exact form that people and ideologies define them. But until we do so, what exactly can there be more than love and the Divine to count as genuine meanings in life and in this world? As stated above, love and the Divine are your meaning in life and in this world, only that you should study and identify these through your intelligent human reasoning, if you are studying the intelligent human meaning and not through beliefs, as you may find everywhere, throughout all studying material and ideologies provided by society. And this is exactly the difference between empirical and intelligent study, because empirical study considers appearances and results, while intelligent research considers entire lines of causality and not only results, replacing appearances and beliefs in this manner with entire models that are capable to explain everything.

And where exactly can you find research material considering reasoning, genuine, accurate facts, and entire intelligent models? Nowhere, not in science, and not throughout social, national, religious, and spiritual ideologies, since these are based on beliefs, theories, and consensus, as they state. The topics of needs, meanings, purposes, and destiny are highly complex, demanding accurate, cognitive, social, real, and existential knowledge. And no one knows these, not even science and academia. Psychology is incapable to model intelligent reasoning along with intuitive thinking and algorithmic thinking, including the relationship that these three forms of thinking have with each other. For sociology, society and the entire human civilization stand only at the confluence of the currently accepted ideologies as capitalism, totalitarianism, and communism, which is disguised capitalism today, along with the currently hidden social ideologies sentientism and egoism. While physics knows only one model capable to explain this world, the big bang theory. How exactly can the big bang theory explain or even integrate your meaning in life and in this world, along with all your needs, moods, modes, and destinies? Yet if you do not display this theory whenever you are asked, you cannot pass your exams, you cannot graduate, you cannot take your place in society according to your meaning and expectations in life, and this is as far the mainstream science can take you.

The topic of this book is complex, requiring highly advanced knowledge only to be able to reason through and conceive it into an accurate intelligent mental model, and this is why I have to write this book now toward the end of this entire book series, with over thirty books preceding it, only to pave the way and offer the necessary background knowledge, just because science and the rest of the ideologies approach the topic of the human meaning empirically, through beliefs, which are ideological, scientific, and philosophical. But can the human meaning ever be hijacked? Causing you to serve others, instead of fulfilling your human meaning?

Love is a relevant meaning in life, yet when you study it minutely, you find love to be a reward feeling, part of your punishment-reward cognitive mechanism, given to you by Life, through your cognitive system, for managing to live your life in the most adequate manner rendering you meaningful and successful, and therefore rendering you capable to fulfill your meaning in life and in this world. In other words, once you remain meaningful, successful, and fulfilling throughout life, you feel only love and happiness. And if anyone or anything hijacks your human meaning, you are not rewarded intrinsically anymore with love and happiness, you lack fulfillment, and you have to take drugs to compensate. Does it seem familiar?

As you already notice, meaning precedes love on all lifelines of causality. Which makes love an effect of your meaning fulfillment. Which might not be too important in general, yet at the third intelligent human level, you distinguish it clearly. Since once you chase love, you end up addicted, at the zero developmental level. But once you chase the fulfillment of your human meaning naturally, through your own intrinsic needs, meanings, feeling, and fulfillment, then you have love and happiness as intrinsic rewards, in very large amounts.

While if you fulfill your meanings at the third intelligent human level, your love and happiness are of the third level, of a very good quality. As a reference, if you have made it so far in the book, it means that you are able to follow it with ease, while reasoning continuously alongside it, fulfilling your third level needs for learning and development the entire time. Which is part of your human meaning. While being rewarded with third level love and happiness the entire time. Since meaning precedes love.

More precisely, love alone is not exactly your meaning in life, but love is only your reward for achieving your meaning in life. Love is also your motivation for you to keep on behaving exactly as you currently do, because you are doing right. Or this is always the case when you feel the feeling of love. And the more intense this feeling of love is, the better you are at what you are doing. But if pain, misery, and hangover follow, than you have it wrong the entire time, since this is the zero addicted level, with pain and hangovers. While that is not love, but pleasure, since there is a difference.

Therefore, you should not seek love directly throughout life, as a feeling, or you end up addicted. But you should seek to fulfill your meaning in life and in this world directly, and if you feel love then, this means that you are doing it right. And if you feel nothing, or worse, if you feel hate instead, then you should stop what you are doing, because you are doing everything wrong.

Do you see how you should not stop directly the feeling of hate either, but you should simply find out what you are doing wrong for your cognitive system to punish you with hate, stop that, and if your hate also stops, then this means that at least you are not behaving against Life and the Divine, against your meaning in life and in this world.

Because you are not exactly bad, guilty, or incapable just because you feel hate, as ideologies claim, but you are only responsible to stop whatever you are doing that generates the feeling of hate. You have to find a different manner in which you fulfill your needs and meanings, and in this manner stop hate and have your love back. Because love and hate are there only to motivate you, since they are simply second level feelings. While you have to use your third level cognitive abilities in order to find a way to be capable to identify, reason through, find the best way, and therefore fulfill your meaning in life and in this world. While you may do so only at an intelligent human level.

Why only at an intelligent human level? Why do you need intelligent human abilities only to be able to fulfill your meanings in life and in this world? Because you are a human being, you have intelligent human potential since this is why you are here, to develop it and use it, and therefore to use it in order to fulfill your intelligent human meaning in life and in this world. Otherwise, Life would have brought a sheep, a worm, a lion, or an elephant in your place to do the job. But she brought you, an intelligent human being, because your intelligent human abilities happen to be compatible to your meaning, and this is what she seeks.

And it is not too difficult to develop yourself to the third level, which is the intelligent human level. Children develop themselves to the third intelligent human level whenever they happen to live in an intelligent human environment. Since you may still find parents in this world capable to provide to their children and to their entire family an intelligent human environment, which is the family itself. This is how these children develop now up to the intelligent human level, even from a young age. And it is only later on, when they discover drugs, ideologies, servitude, and even hierarchic brotherhoods, that they decay in development, down to the first servitude level and even zero addicted level.

While their parents remain unaware of this entire, highly complex cognitive process. Because if it was not for the Consensual Matrix with all its ideologies, then everybody developed at the intelligent human level throughout childhood, to make this world an intelligent human place.

But how exactly does the Consensual Matrix stop your development? Does the Consensual Matrix come in the bedroom of your child to access the Internet there, to light up their first cigarette, or to determine them to participate in their first organized crime? Well, yes, it is the Consensual Matrix involved in this last example, but the Consensual Matrix is the one providing drugs to all children and not only to your child. And then it is the same Consensual Matrix advertising for all drugs in all movies and songs everywhere in society, and even at school and in cartoons. And it is impossible to develop to your intelligent human level anymore in this kind of environment, since it is of a very low level, and since you must always match your environment in order to be able to cope with it. Therefore, your cognitive system decays rapidly to the level of your new environment, matching it. And so you become part of the Consensual Matrix, since on lower developmental levels, you cannot reason anymore, but you need beliefs to think through. This is how you adopt entire ideologies, good or bad, whatever happens to be around, and so you continue living your life, on lower developmental levels, within the Consensual Matrix. And now your entire lower level behavior maintains a lower level environment all around, it affects negatively everybody else, since you share that environment with everybody else, this vicious existential circle goes on, and the Consensual Matrix has you the entire time, to continue in this manner throughout the ages, indefinitely.

Yet as you already notice, humanity develops slowly, it already nibbles on the most common intelligent human needs and meanings, many people already start avoiding drugs systematically, many already start distinguishing the Consensual Matrix and its consensual meaning in this world, or at least its most visible structure, and this is how entire nations gain their freedom from the invisible kingdom and from the tyrants and dictators of the East today, very slowly. And who knows, the Consensual Matrix as you know it, might not be around several centuries from now. If your genetic line happens to still be around then, and not already exterminated by the invisible kingdom and the dictators of the East, since this is the agenda. And when only the invisible kingdom or the dictators of the East are left in this world, then the Consensual Matrix has no purpose anymore to enslave the people, since they are the only ones around then, one supreme, 'superior' genetic line, in the entire world. Or this is what they are promised, since the Consensual Matrix uses them just as it uses everybody today.

How exactly can you tell truth from lies and promises? Are genuinely developed humans capable to use their intelligent human cognitive abilities in order to escape this kind of existential schemes? Many times, all that you have to do is maintain yourself at an intelligent human developmental level, adopt in this manner an intelligent human behavior and lifestyle, and through them, manage to fulfill your genuine human meaning in life and in this world. And through this specific intelligent human meaning, you create throughout life and throughout this world an intelligent human environment, which stands above the Consensual Matrix and all its consensual characteristics. And always rely on your feelings as assurance, since the primal intelligences of your cognitive system that send you your needs and feelings are integral part of Life and Intelligence, they have been in these circumstances countless of times throughout your genetic line, and now they truly know what they do and what they demand from you. As they want the best for you.

Because you may know when you are truly fulfilling your genuine meaning, by using your intelligent human reasoning and awareness, while you also know it through the feelings that you receive as a reward from your cognitive system. Since you feel only love and happiness then, and nothing else. And this is significant to identify, because when love is over, when you cannot feel love anymore, or even worse, when all that you feel is hate and this goes against all your principles and understandings in life, when you cannot help it but hate what once used to be the love of your life, as it is the case with couples before divorce, with old cars and houses that need to be replaced, or with irrelevant jobs that stand in your way, in these dreadful circumstances of pure hate. You do not really need slogans, motivation material, incantations, meditations, along with the rest of the beliefs and ideologies to bring back love in your life, since they never do, but they only postpone the worst. And this is the case because Life and the Divine give you a specific meaning and you should always follow it, or you receive hate at first, only to help you stabilize, by pushing you away from your inadequate behavior. And when you do not listen, you go down from there, if you do not behave as you feel, if you do not do as expected.

And as you notice, love and the rest of your feelings are not enough to reveal your true meaning in life explicitly, because you still have to reason accurately in order to identify what goes on in your life and why exactly your cognitive system sends you these specific feelings. Because it is never your direct implication in everything concerning your natural feelings, good and bad, including love and hate, because you are simply a receiver in everything that you feel, not a creator of these feelings yourself. And therefore, you should always guide and adjust your behavior according to your feelings, and not the other way around, as people always tend to do. More precisely, you do not have to seek directly your good feelings and avoid the worst, but you have to seek to identify and fulfill your needs, and through them, your meanings, since the intelligences of your cognitive system reward you with your good feelings when you succeed. Or if you ever fail your needs and meanings, then the same intelligences punish you through dreadful feelings.

As a reference, love is an inner cognitive reward for a long-term achievement or for a long-term system of achievements, while hate means stop doing what you are doing, because it is not relevant anymore, it already goes against your meaning, and it can become even harmful if you do not stop it now. You did everything perfectly so far, you have received your love accordingly, but now the outside environment has probably changed, or you have changed, or she has changed, or plans have changed, and now you have to adjust your behavior once again, according to Life and to your cognitive system, in order to keep on following your meaning in life.

As a reference, it happens that Life, humanity, and your specific genetic line want to achieve an abundant, strong, and highly diverse genetic background, and you can never achieve these by having only one partner or spouse for life, as society and the multitude of ideologies controlling society demand, enforce, and expect. You must have a multitude of partners, for a strong, diverse genetic background, partners who must also have a multitude of partners, all connected through natural love, since only Life knows what specific genes match and complete what specific genes. And you should follow them closely, by following your love and desires freely, because this is why you receive them. If not, you fail your meaning in life, again, which this time is to reproduce successfully throughout life. And you know it well, because all punishments related to your reproductive meaning in life and in this world have never ceased to leave you alone your entire life, just because you have been failing this reproductive meaning your entire life. Or this is the case unless you already have six children or more to tell the story, all well taken care of and well educated. But if you have only two, one, or none at all, you simply kill your own genetic line.

What about religious beliefs, moral codes, and overpopulation? Look around, to see all nations that have implemented successfully contraceptive measures and beliefs through all means and ideologies in order to avoid overpopulation are going slowly extinct today, just because the multitude of genetic lines to have composed them once, go slowly extinct. And now, all these nations have to open their doors to immigrants, if they are still lucky to be chosen by these incoming masses of people. Because if not, and if contraceptive measures persist, and if immigrants stop coming, then these nations die away from the inside out, starting with isolated, remote communities that lose all inhabitants at first, then continuing with the most unsuccessful cities to lose all their citizens. Until the entire nation loses its people, either through death and old age, or through emigration. Gangs move in, and nothing that happens there remains relevant to Life and to the Divine. Everything falls in nonexistence, and it does not count as part of Life and the Divine anymore, but only as part of the Consensual Matrix. And this might already explain Earth today and in the near future, along with this entire world.

The masses of incoming people that happen to favor developed nations today come from poorer nations that were and probably still are milder in everything concerning reproduction. And this is why they still have an abundant population today, formed by abundant, diverse genetic lines. Or this was the case until recently, because now, the entire world suffers under strong contraceptive measures and under strong moral codes, and this is how the entire world goes down the drain.

Because Life and the Divine never forgive you and never look twice before removing you from existence, for failing one need, one meaning, which is this case with reproduction. And since today, contraceptive measures are implemented deliberately, only to exterminate unwanted genetic lines, which happens to be almost the entire world, and since it is always you implementing these strong moral codes of contraceptive measures to your own family, to your own children, to your own genetic line, and to everyone around, then Life and the Divine might be the ones taking you out along with your entire genetic line, just as you persist to instate. While I noticed how the more you fulfill first level consensual needs and meanings, the more Life takes you out. Because this is how the Consensual Matrix pushes you under the bus of Life.

What do science, ideologies, education, and media teach you about your own meaning in life and in this world? Let us see. Cults, religions, and spirituality teach you in general the same thing, to seek the Divine, find the Divine, be with the Divine, and serve the Divine, eternally. Spirituality encourages you to seek the Divine, Life, this world, and yourself, to find higher knowledge about yourself, about Life, Intelligence, and about this world. While all these are meanings of the third, human level and higher, and you may achieve them through your natural, intelligent human needs and meanings. However, when you study the specific meaning in life that many ideologies demand from you, you find them diverging from your natural, genuine meaning in life, in society, and in this world. And this is exactly why there are tens of thousands of cults, religions, and schools of thought today, each one demanding from you a different behavior. While there should be only one behavior associated to your genuine meaning in life and in this world, the intelligent human behavior, capable to define and fulfill your entire human meaning. Even more, by diverting you from your intelligent human behavior, they divert you from fulfilling your intelligent human meaning. And since you are not even capable to define your intelligent human meaning in life and in this world but through ideological beliefs, as you find them currently in science and in this world, now you are incapable to differentiate the good from the bad yourself, you do not know what to do, and this is how you fall into servitude under the common hierarchies and authorities of society. And this now defines your human meaning, the consensual one, the only one.

What exactly defines your meanings today according to everybody else? Just have a look throughout your favorite encyclopedia to see it for yourself. Here is a small compendium of what I found at a first glance online, stated in italics. We start with meanings of life and meanings in life and in this world, found in popular and literary sources:

"To realize one's potential and ideals."

As you may notice, this first meaning is not exactly a meaning in life, but it is a need, a third level intelligent human need. The difference between meanings and needs is that meanings are wider and comprehensive, made of countless of needs standing at the base of all meanings, making meanings and destinies possible as a whole, one fulfillment at a time. And this is exactly why in your favorite encyclopedia, you do not find exactly the meaning of life, the meaning of this world, or your meaning in life and it this world, but you find enumerations of slogans and rimes, with a few needs, and even consensual beliefs along with beautiful words, everything that people found significant enough in one era or another to pursue and be fulfilled throughout life.

This is what people believe, and therefore this is what people now state. Because science, education, and people in general cannot distinguish between the empirical study that they do, and the intelligent research that could have helped them find all genuine meanings and destinies, as far as human abilities allow. Because people cannot distinguish between simple thinking and genuine reasoning, between beliefs and genuine facts, or between truth and validity or consensus.

Because science and education have never found this topic relevant enough to consider teaching. And this is why you find debates today replacing genuine research and understanding. Consequently, now you lack pertinent understanding yourself, and now you have to consent to these not through truth and facts, but through opinions, intuitive thinking, debates, and common sense. And these are of lower cognitive level, far below the intelligent human reasoning. While they also keep you in lower developmental levels.

Can you realize your full potential in this manner throughout life? But who or what exactly defines your true potential? Your ideologies? Your jurisdictions? Your teachers and the entire education? Because if your true potential is to accumulate more beliefs in your cognitive system, as many as it takes, then you never develop to your intelligent human level. And you can never develop to your intelligent human level through beliefs, common sense, intuitive thinking, and general opinions and consensus, since these are easily hijacked, and you end up working and living your life for others, under their tight control, while probably believing the entire time that you are free. And these others will make sure that you never develop cognitively, in order for you to remain always under their command, along with your entire genetic line following you, since this is always the case and you may see it throughout history. And as you notice, we are already eons away, while it is still going on unchanged. You can realize your full potential only at the intelligent human level, through sustained development, allowing a genuine, intelligent reasoning based on a solid awareness of all genuine facts. I study these subjects throughout a multitude of books of this series.

We may assume here that full potential means full development, which is the intelligent human development and more, if you are ever able to take yourself further. To consider this first intelligent human need, the need for continuous development and therefore the need for realizing your full potential and ideals, you always have to seek and realize your full potential throughout life and you may do so only through an accurate, consistent development to the intelligent human level and beyond, with results depending on your environment, expectations, social status, abilities, and determinations.

Can you realize your ideals when you achieve to realize your full potential? Well, you may do anything once you achieve your full human potential, at the intelligent human level. Yet ideals tend to be consensual in nature, and you might end up investing your entire full potential into consensual meanings, whatever these ideals state. You may find this case within the current hierarchic Brotherhood, among its lower layers, while coincidentally, this specific statement is always acclaimed there as an intelligent human meaning.

Let us move now to the next 'meaning' from the encyclopedia. Notice that these first meanings are simple, common, popular, and literary meanings found all around.

"To chase dreams."

This is another empirical statement, to chase dreams, which is, to go where no one has ever gone before, or to try persistently everything out of the ordinary that may seem relevant. While all intelligent human needs are natural and therefore intrinsic, sent to you directly by Life and by the Divine through all intelligences of your cognitive system, opposed to all consensual needs sent to you through beliefs or through direct orders, coming from the Consensual Matrix through the multitude of all its beliefs, codes of law, social expectations, and ideologies. We study closely how everything is done in the next chapter, since the second chapter of this book is mostly cognitive and therefore conceptual in nature. While I keep all first chapters of all books of this series at an empirical perspective, for a better understanding.

Because you chase dreams, I chase dreams, we chase dreams when it is possible, when we have the time and the means, and when we are allowed. But what exactly does it mean to chase dreams? How do we do so? Through what human abilities? For what purpose? How does everything take place at the social and cognitive levels? Because until you answer these in an accurate manner, you cannot understand your true meaning in life.

Why exactly do you have to know your meaning in life? To make a point? To be specific and correct? To have a quintessential validation that everything that you do is correct? Yes, even if they are purely empiric. However, without knowing why you are here and what you have to do, then anyone may claim anything as a meaning for you, you fall for it, and so you are determined to engage in anything that they please, serving them for now or even indefinitely, even without your knowledge. You may harm yourself and this world in this manner, you miss your life opportunities, and this world is full of examples to state. Or the entire world is a big example to state.

How exactly can you tell that what you do is good or bad, if it is with you or against you, if it is with this world or against this world? This is the question. Because without knowing the exact human meaning, you cannot answer it, and you cannot distinguish the good from the bad on your own. You cannot distinguish the good from the bad yourself, and this is why you have to rely on authorities of all kind, on anyone willing to exploit you, anyone who claims to know the truth, the same authorities to have exploited you in this manner this entire time, keeping you in this vicious circle.

And how do you escape this vicious circle? If you chase your dreams and ideas, despite of what your designated ideology states, you fail most of the time, but you still get to step outside your vicious circle of reasoning, sometimes, if only once. And if you succeed, at least once, then you did so, you found yourself out, you broke free of orders and beliefs, free of the Consensual Matrix. Your dream came true at last, you can see and understand this world now, and you can distinguish the good from the bad yourself, if only for a moment, if only for an instant, and you may even catch a glimpse of the true human meaning.

"To live one's dreams."

"To spend it for something that will outlast it."

"To matter: to count, to stand for something, to have made some difference that you lived at all.

"To expand one's potential in life."

"To become the person you've always wanted to be."

"To become the best version of yourself."

"To seek happiness and flourish."

"To be a true authentic human being."

"To be able to put the entire of oneself into one's feelings, one's work, one's beliefs."

"To follow or submit to our destiny."

"To achieve eudaimonia, a flourishing of human spirit."

"To achieve biological perfection."

"To survive, that is, to live as long as possible, including pursuit of immortality (through scientific means)."

"To live forever or die trying."

"Existence, to keep existing, to keep being, to preserve own existence; not to cease to be, not to disappear; existence solely relying on itself; to overcome threats to own existence; existential and ontological self-sufficiency."

"To adapt. Often to improve one's chances of success in another

purpose; sometimes, as a purpose in itself (adapting to adapt)."

"To evolve."

"To replicate, to reproduce. The 'dream' of every cell is to become two cells.

"To seek wisdom and knowledge."

"To expand one's perception of this world."

"To follow the clues and walk out the exit."

"To learn as many things as possible in life."

"To know as much as possible about as many things as possible."

"To seek wisdom and knowledge and to tame the mind, as to avoid suffering caused by ignorance and find happiness."

"To face our fears and accept the lessons life offers us."

"To find the meaning or purpose of life."

"To find a reason to live."

"To resolve the imbalance of the mind by understanding the nature of reality."

"To do good, to do the right thing."

"To leave this world as a better place than you found it."

"To do your best to leave every circumstance better than you found it."

"To benefit others."

"To give more than you take."

"To end suffering."

"To create equality."

"To challenge oppression."

"To distribute wealth."

"To be generous."

"To contribute to the well-being and spirit of others."

"To help others, to help one another."

"To take every chance to help another while on your journey here."

"To be creative and innovative."

"To forgive."

"To accept and forgive human flaws."

"To be emotionally sincere."

"To be responsible."

"To be honorable."

"To seek peace."

The following are meanings relating to religion. I always use the words Deity or Divine, in order to maintain religious neutrality.

"The Deity created death and life to test you [as to] who is best in deed and He is Exalted in Might, the Forgiving."

"To worship the Divine, to enter heaven in afterlife."

"To reach the highest heaven and be at the heart of the Divine."

"To have a pure soul and experience the Divine."

"To understand the mystery of the Divine."

"To know or attain union with the Divine."

"To know oneself, know others, and know the will of heaven."

"To love something bigger, greater, and beyond ourselves, something we did not create or have the power to create, something intangible and made holy by our very belief in it."

"To love the Divine and all of his creations."

"To glorify the Divine by enjoying him forever."

"To spread your religion and share it with others."

"To act justly, love mercy, and walk humbly with your Divine."

"To be fruitful and multiply."

"To obtain freedom."

"To fill the Earth and subdue it."

"To serve humankind, to prepare to meet and become more like the Divine, to choose good over evil, and have joy."

The following are meanings relating to love, and I state them as I found them. Note that you can never choose and determine your feelings directly, at will, since specific intelligences of your cognitive system give you these feelings, as part of your punishment-reward mechanism that they use in order to control your behavior throughout life and throughout the outside environment. You cannot control your love directly, but only through the successful fulfillment of your long-term needs and meanings, as your love for being around specific favorable people, or your love to undergo specific favorable long-term activities. Because if you follow love, pleasure, and happiness directly as it is stated next, you may end up addicted, and examples are many to give. And even so, the following meanings are very beautiful.

"To love, to feel, to enjoy the act of living."

"To love more."

"To love those who mean the most. Every life you touch will touch you back."

"To treasure every enjoyable sensation one has."

"To seek beauty in all its forms."

"To have fun or enjoy life."

"To seek pleasure and avoid pain."

"To be compassionate."

"To be moved by the tears and pain of others, and try to help them out of love and compassion."

"To love others as best possibly."

"To eat, drink, and be merry."

The following meanings are of a social nature. Most of these are still slogans, simple needs, along with consensual beliefs, and therefore they are of the second level, and not intelligent human needs, which are of the third level. The second level is the animal level, and even though animals do not form complex societies as humans do, they still abide by the same social needs that humans have, just because animals live life alongside a multitude of animals, and these are the social needs controlling their group, school, pack, or herd behavior throughout life, as needs of social acceptance, social competition, social supremacy, social security, social exploitation, and social extermination.

However, all social needs are part of your cognitive system, and you can still receive them under specific circumstances, including the specific need of becoming a dictator and ruling large groups of people as a dictator. Yet once you develop to your intelligent human level, your need for wellbeing and righteousness in this world surpasses your need for social competition, social supremacy, social injustice, social discrimination, and tyranny, just because at your third developmental level, your meaning changes to the intelligent human meaning.

"To have power, to be better."

"To strive for power and superiority."

"To rule this world."

"To know and master this world."

"To know and master nature."

The following meanings are about experiencing everything as is, as it comes, or the absence of all meanings. These are relevant to state here, since these are meanings that science, education, and society propagate. Note that science enters in contradiction here not only with religious ideologies as it is commonly known, but it enters in contradiction with everything. Since it is characteristic to science, to education, and to society to make you believe that everything about you is irrelevant, insignificant, and minimized in life and in this world, including your place and meaning in life and in this world. And everything is done for specific agendas that you may now easily distinguish.

"Life has no meaning."

"Life or human existence has no real meaning or purpose because human existence occurred out of a random chance in nature, and anything that exists by chance has no intended purpose."

"Life has no meaning, but as humans we try to associate a meaning or purpose so we can justify our existence."

"There is no point in life, and that is exactly what makes it so special."

"One should not seek to know and understand the meaning of life."

"The answer to the meaning of life is too profound to be known and understood."

"You will never live if you are looking for the meaning of life."

"The meaning of life is to forget about the search for the meaning of life."

"Ultimately, a person should not ask what the meaning of their life is, but rather must recognize that it is they themselves who are asked. In a word, each person is questioned by life; and they can only answer to life by answering for their own life; to life they can only respond by being responsible."

The following meanings regard negative interpretations of all meanings. They are relevant to state here in order to highlight specific ideologies that use them in order to change the good into bad and the bad into good, for various purposes and agendas.

"Life is bad."

"Better never to have been."

"People will always experience pain (harm) which outweighs any pleasure. Not coming into existence means people will not experience pain, nor will they be disadvantaged by not experiencing pleasure, as these do not exist. This is described as the asymmetry of pleasure and pain."

2 NEEDS AND MEANINGS

Now you know everything about your meaning in everything, just by reading the slogans and rimes above. Beautiful slogans. But how exactly do intelligences send you needs and meanings? How are they capable to determine you to do everything that you do throughout life? And how exactly are Life and the Divine capable to send you needs, meanings, and feelings through your intelligences or through your cognitive system? And how can they do so not only to humans, but to all animals? And you want to know all these and much more not empirically, not in beautiful words and rimes as given above, not through believes, but you want to know it from cognitive and intelligent perspectives, which is, you want to know it exactly as it takes place in your mind. How exactly can your mind hold your intelligences and how can they send you needs and feelings from there? Because if you can understand this, you may understand your life and meanings in this world, and therefore you may be able to distinguish the good from the bad on your own, just by following your natural needs and feelings, if you are ever able to separate them from your first level consensual needs and dogma. Let us see.

Cognition relates to minds and intelligences, and to your consciousness. Psychology uses the term consciousness frequently, yet it has it poorly modeled. Therefore, you may distinguish now two human intelligences, your conscious intelligence and your subconscious intelligence, while your cognitive system is filled with intelligences of all kind. I refer to your mind as your cognitive system, only that your cognitive system spans not only your brain, but your entire physical body. Are there more than two intelligences in your cognitive system? Yes, and they are intelligent, since all intelligences are conscious, they interact with their immediate environment, they have definite tasks in this world, they think and reason depending on their own developmental level, they have and send needs and feelings, and therefore they have meanings in their life and in their immediate world.

Who is who in your cognitive system? Psychology simply splits the human mind in two: the conscious, and the unconscious or subconscious minds. What is the difference between the subconscious and the unconscious? There are certainly definitions for these, they might be similar in principle, and this is about all that psychology can state. How do you reason, memorize, feel, need, and perceive? Psychology does not know, but it still wonders of how incredible the human mind is. And therefore, psychology cannot ever attempt to study and understand the topic of this book, the human meaning. Is this done on purpose?

Consciousness is the specific part of your cognitive system that you are able to access and therefore use and control at will, in a conscious manner. While the subconscious and the unconscious make for the rest. Psychology fails to identify a multitude of discrete, unique, independent intelligences residing in the subconscious and unconscious part of your cognitive system.

Are you capable to learn and understand everything you desire? Yes, and you may do so yourself, consciously, through your own conscious intelligence. Because from among your entire cognitive system, you can identify yourself as the conscious intelligence. Can you digest your last meal on your own, as a conscious intelligence? No, but you ate that meal on your own as a conscious intelligence, and hopefully it counts. Did you send your own need, your hunger to do so too? No, you just felt hungry, you ate your dinner, everything digests now nicely on its own in your stomach, and this is how it happened.

How exactly did it happen? Who is digesting your meal now, because it is an extremely difficult job to take your proteins apart one amino acid after another, molecule by molecule, while the laws of chemistry are not enough to do so? Someone does so, there in your stomach, someone intelligent and certainly conscious, digesting your nutrients one molecule at a time, then transporting them to trillions of cells exactly as they need, while still sending some nutrients for storage within particular specialized cells, for future times of hunger when they will be well needed throughout the body. Who does so? No one, as science claims, everything is done randomly and or mechanically, it has always been done in this manner, and your entire organism and species achieved to do so throughout the ages, through trial and error, randomly, through the survival of the fittest, and through evolution.

Or this is what this ideology called science keeps claiming one century after another, which is not true at all. There is a highly powerful, highly pertinent intelligence right now within your own cognitive system sending you specific needs of exactly what you have to eat, in the exact amount to last you until the next meal or until the next week when you go shopping again, depending on the nutrient in cause. This is your primal eating subconscious intelligence. You may identify all your primal intelligences by the needs that they send you. You may even see them at work throughout the body, once you know where to look.

Your entire cognitive system is divided into primal intelligences. Primal intelligences are also divided into a multitude of inner intelligences, which are divided into further inner, inner intelligences, as far down as cognitive processes require. You as a conscious intelligence are one of them, a primal intelligence, and you live in your cognitive system along with your primal social intelligence, primal reproductive intelligence, primal security intelligence, primal recovery intelligence, and primal excretion intelligence. And together, you form your cognitive system.

As you notice, your primal intelligences are specialized within your cognitive system and therefore within your organism, and this specialization is exactly their meaning in their immediate environment, throughout life, throughout their life. And this is the difference between needs and meanings for all intelligences and living beings, since you always fulfill needs for yourself, while you fulfill meanings for everybody else.

It is enough to scan your cognitive system right now, to be able to perceive or feel all your intelligences, through the multitude of your needs, feelings, instincts, and traits. And as you are capable to identify them now, you are capable to maintain the inner harmony of your cognitive system, just as you are capable to maintain harmony in your outside environments, in your family environment, working environment, entourage of friends, neighborhood, community, nation, and society.

You know all tasks and meanings of all your primal intelligences, but what is your own task or specialization within your organism and cognitive system as a conscious intelligence? Because whatever it is, that is your meaning within your organism and cognitive system, and you must know it well. Your specialization as a conscious intelligence is to monitor, control, and manage the activity of your entire organism as it interacts with the outside world, in order to fulfill your needs. You are more as a driver and operator, yet it takes more than movement skills while interacting with the outside world. And you notice the difference between needs and meanings, since meanings are only one for each environment, and they relate mostly to specializations that you have in these environments. Through your specific meaning or specialization, you work for that specific environment. While you are capable to fulfill your own needs in that environment, in a win-win relationship with your environment.

You have a multitude of environments as a human being, besides your body environment and mind environment. You have your natural environment with pristine mountains and forests, along with your family environment, work environment, social environment, friends environment, and brotherhood environment. You notice that your natural and family environments are genuine or natural, while the Consensual Matrix might have the rest, along with the entire society. And then you have your Internet environment, videogames environment, and higher environment with all souls and higher beings. While you have a meaning to fulfill throughout life in all these environments, and you certainly have to be able to identify it, tend to it, and therefore fulfill it. Because others depend on you in each environment, and if you fulfill all these meanings for all these environments randomly or instinctually, it might not be enough, and therefore you fail your meaning. And because you fail, now the entire environment suffers, or fails. Which is the case right now with our world, so important, that it takes everybody to the common grave. And with many human genetic lines already there.

Why interacting with the outside world? You need to intake resources, to have shelter, clothing, transportation, and proper temperature. You have to learn and to be around specific people and partners in order to interact in particular manners, and it is certainly more complicated than you now assume. And you can never do so if you are not using your reasoning at its best, otherwise you fail your needs, since life on Earth is very competitive today.

Just study your behavior briefly now, to see how everything that you do in life, you do in order to fulfill your needs. As a reference, you take drugs in order to fulfill needs of the zero level, which are needs for pure pleasure. Yet you may get your pleasure, love, happiness, along with the rest of your good feeling as rewards every time you fulfill your needs and meanings of all levels, and therefore you do not have to take drugs. Only that when you do not receive your rewards for various reasons, for having all your needs already taken care of and fulfilled for you, then you tend to crave for your good feelings. And so you take your drugs, and you go down from there, straight down to the zero developmental level. While it is more likely that you never get up again. Because everybody takes drugs, while today, even doctors encourage you to do so, and they even give you more drugs to take. And this is part of the Consensual Matrix, in order to keep you down, weak, and on lower developmental levels.

Or if you want your good feelings right away, you may simply engage in any activity that is easier to fulfill, as eating unnecessarily because you are bored, and this is how people gain weight. Because they are bored, and because they cannot understand their needs and feelings, mistaking their needs along with their fulfillment.

But what exactly can you do in order to avoid drugs and still receive your good feelings? This is the question, because when you have a human society filled with failures, sickness, and addictions, something is going on. The current society is not a human society, but a consensual, exploiting environment, similar to any work camp that you may find anywhere.

While humans need intelligent human environments in order to subsist at their own developmental level. Because your environment must always match your mind, abilities, meanings, needs, expectations. And your environment must match these through its environmental lifestyle and conditions that it has to offer, while on your turn, you have to match all these with your own human behavior, only to be able to fulfill your needs and meanings.

This does not mean that all human beings should be born within advanced university campuses where they get to learn and perform genuine art and science since birth for the rest of their lives, even though this seems to be a proper human environment. But humans may start with any natural environment, as low as it is, because through their human needs and therefore through their intelligent human behavior demanded by their human needs, humans are capable to change their environment in the exact manner rendering it an intelligent human environment, achieving to be able to fulfill in this manner their meaning in that specific environment.

And this would be the case with this world, in society, if humans were allowed to change it into an intelligent human environment. This is never the case in society, which is the main human environment, a social environment, because society is not a natural human social environment, but it is a consensual environment, forcefully constrained to remain on very low and very unfavorable developmental levels, on purpose, through the multitude of laws and ideologies that you already know.

And this is why you are not capable or you are not allowed to fulfill the multitude of your intelligent human needs throughout life. You might not even know your intelligent human needs in order to be able to identify them now when you receive them, while your cognitive system still sends you these human needs, as long as your environment remains below your innate standards. You do not identify them, you do not fulfill them, but you fulfill very low level needs instead. And it never works out right, you never receive your love and happiness as rewards. Yet you still receive some love and happiness from the fulfillment of your second level animal needs, it is not enough, you substitute with drugs since everybody does so, and you go down from there. Even more, your cognitive system still punishes you for not fulfilling the multitude of your human needs that it sends to you, and this makes matters worse. And if you happen to be a highly evolved soul on top of all these, coming here in this world with a full list of higher level demands and expectations, then good luck to you.

In general, the multitude of your needs and their continuous fulfillment is enough to keep you pleased and happy throughout life, only that a great part of your needs are missing today, removed systematically and deliberately from your life, lifestyle, and behavior. These are your genuine developmental human needs, and this is exactly why you cannot even enumerate more than one or a few human needs now, while they are countless. Because they are systematically removed from your lifestyle, only to keep you within the Consensual Matrix, for life. All humans were supposed to fulfill human needs throughout life, since they are human, while animals are supposed to remain engaged in the fulfillment of their animal needs throughout life, which are the well-known physiological needs, plus the social and security needs. You also share with all animals these second level needs, while society was supposed to offer the fulfillment of all these lower, second level animal needs to you by default, since this is exactly why you live your life in society. While you were supposed to remain determined throughout life to fulfill your intelligent human needs, fulfilling in this manner your genuine meaning in life and in this world. And throughout this entire higher level human fulfillment, you were supposed to receive all your love, happiness, and pleasure that you could ever have, every moment of your life.

Is this the case in your life? Yes, for now, as long as you read this book, because this happens to be an intelligent human activity, which is the fulfillment of your human need for higher learning and therefore higher development. But how often do you have the chance to fulfill your intelligent human needs throughout life? How much learning material are you capable to find at the intelligent human level to study and develop? Not much. While higher learning is but one of the multitude of human needs. And what does the Consensual Matrix do now? It feeds you drugs to make up for the missing love, happiness, and pleasure that you were supposed to receive naturally at the third intelligent human level, and it does not really work. Because drugs cannot exactly give you love and happiness, but only pleasure, temporarily, before everything changes to pain, misery, and discomfort, all the way down to exasperation, madness, and suicide. Yet people still take drugs, in every manner, and it probably makes no difference anyway at underdeveloped levels.

Boredom is highly important to understand here, since

boredom is not exactly your need for pleasure and entertainment as society, media, and entertainment make you believe, but when you feel bored, you are actually failing your developmental needs, which are higher level needs. Boredom is the mild punishment that you receive for failing your learning and developmental needs, and these may be as high as the intelligent human level, and higher. While needs at this third developmental level are difficult to identify and fulfill. And therefore, it is by far easier for you to take pleasure from drugs and entertainment instead, and this is what the Consensual Matrix recommends that you should do, along with all your friends and the entire society. Not that the Consensual Matrix is ever capable to allow you the fulfillment of your higher human needs and meanings.

At the first developmental level, you have all your servitude needs. These belong to the Consensual Matrix, since the entire first level development is consensual in nature, just as the zero developmental level, both being part of the Consensual Matrix. And many times, you integrate in society through servitude, you enter straight into the tight hierarchies that society has to offer, you serve others from there while fewer below serve you, you refer to this as your social interaction or job environment, while everything is part of the Consensual Matrix. And this is how you get to live your life if you are not careful, at the first developmental level, as part of the Consensual Matrix.

As a reference, the entire current Brotherhood is of the first developmental level, along with the entire invisible kingdom. The Masses are more fortunate to be able to reach the second developmental level toward its upper social layers. And who knows, there might still be people within the Masses aspiring to their third developmental level, currently preoccupied with the fulfillment of their intelligent human needs. You can even find their drawings, books, and videos online.

Yet developmental levels are not exactly a prerequisite for this life. And even more, your cognitive system sends you developmental needs in order for you to develop according to your environment and to your expectations, not according to a mandatory list of objectives: first you develop to the zero level when you are little, then you develop to the first level shortly after, then to the second developmental level in the fifth grade, and then to the human level shortly after. This is not how development takes place, because the natural development starts with the second, animal level. While in the current society, you are not expected to develop to your intelligent human level, but you are only expected to match your environment with your development, with your abilities, with your responsibility and reasoning, and therefore with your behavior.

However, if society was an intelligent human society of the third developmental level, then everybody would have pushed you persistently to develop to your intelligent human level, in order to match everybody else. Otherwise, you altered their highly developed environment if even slightly, and they could certainly tell. And this is the case because as we will see throughout the book, as long as you live in an intelligent human society, you have to fulfill a specific social meaning throughout life, a specific social specialization, serving in this manner your environment. This is your main meaning in society and in this world, while this is a third level meaning, or a human meaning. If you are of a lower developmental level, then you cannot fulfill it, this world still depends on you if only slightly, and therefore the entire world pushes you now to develop accordingly, in order for you to be able to do your job, to fulfill your meaning. And many times, it is this unique circumstance pushing you to develop throughout life, adding in this manner to the multitude of developmental needs that your own primal intelligences send you.

What should you do? Should you develop or not throughout life? Is it tedious to develop? It is easy for you in particular, since you are already developing as you read. However, you may do anything else instead throughout life, since society allows it. It only happens that you are a human being, and you are supposed to fulfill your intelligent human needs, while living your life at the intelligent human level, within a genuine natural human environment, while fulfilling your intelligent human meaning within society and within the natural world. Do you? Because important human needs are the need for freedom, along with the need for self-reliance, wellbeing, independent development, and independent reasoning. And through the fulfillment of all human needs, you always stand above the Consensual Matrix, above all hierarchies of society, and above the current hierarchic Brotherhood, while fulfilling your natural, intelligent human meanings. Because when you fail your meaning in society, then everybody else suffers, exactly as you suffer while you lack the means to fulfill your own intelligent human needs. And it happens in this manner because others as you fail to fulfill their intelligent human meaning in society, affecting others who fail in this manner to fulfill their intelligent human needs and meanings, in a vicious circle. And this is how you fail to find pertinent learning material to teach you about Life, about this world, about yourself, and about your place and meaning in life and in this world, because others as you had failed to provide it throughout their life. You fail to have pertinent politicians representing you in society, because they had already joined the Consensual Matrix and went corrupt. You fail to have proper, genuine food to help you develop, because the Consensual Matrix feeds you poison, while doctors, along with everyone working in the food industry never care about you or even work against you, on purpose. And this is how you fail to have an entire intelligent human environment keeping you on higher developmental levels, but only lies, conflicts, discrimination, and harassment. And this is how you learn to do the same.

We will study about your meanings of higher levels and higher and social classes throughout the book. What we want to know now is how your primal intelligences live, behave, and interact within your cognitive system. Are they more as little electric snakes and worms in there, shooting impressively from one neuron to another throughout axons and dendrites? Yes, you may see them in this manner on EEG displays if you can, yet this is how you see them from here, from the perspective of this world. While all your intelligences live their lives in the inner world of your cognitive system, and this inner cognitive world is relatively different than the outside world. Even more, you as a conscious intelligence live in the inner world of your mind, an inner world that is a replica of the outside world. And you live in there as the inner self, and not as the actual physical organism, which lives in the outside world.

As an inner self, you are also confusing the outside world with your inner world, just because you perceive and understand everything from the outside world through your inner world. There is always a discrepancy between the two worlds, the outside world and the inner world. And this leads to all disagreements that you have with people around, because you perceive and understand the outside world in different manners, through your own abilities, inner worlds, and inner selves. Or this is the case if you live your life on lower developmental levels, since this is how you engage in first level debates instead of third level intelligent reasoning.

But how different is your inner replica of this world from the outside world? Just start drawing or painting right now, and that is how accurate your inner world is, compared to the outside world. And now, when you add the beliefs of all ideologies interacting with your cognitive system, your inner replica of this world might be even more inaccurate than that. And everything impacts on your ability to fulfill your meanings, it happens to everybody, and this is how the entire world decays. And now you cannot understand your own primal intelligences and how they send you your needs, if you do not understand yourself as a primal conscious intelligence living within your cognitive system, within your inner mind world. I study this subject throughout a multitude of books of this series, since understanding your intelligences along with their cognitive activity is relevant to understanding yourself.

Everything that you do in life you do in order to fulfill your needs and meanings. As we have seen, there are countless of tasks happening right now within your organism, performed by other intelligences, and they do them by far better than you can as a conscious intelligence. You cannot filter blood within kidneys at a conscious level, or digest and store fatty acids better than your primal intelligences can, while they cannot interact with the outside world better than you do. This is why all intelligences of your cognitive system tend to all inner tasks of your organism. And if there are tasks that they cannot do themselves, as tasks of interaction with the outside world, they pass them to you as needs, expecting their immediate fulfillment. You feel these needs, you identify them, you reason, you find out first how to fulfill them, you decide what to do about it and how to do so, and then you do so right away, or you wait for the proper time.

Visiting the bathroom is a simple example here, yet many times, you cannot visit the bathroom immediately when your primal excretion intelligence sends you the need, but you have to wait for the end of the class, or you have to wait to stop the car. And many times, your primal intelligences cooperate with you fully, your excretion intelligence learns your schedule accurately, and asks you to visit the bathroom immediately when you get back home, and not at work or during bus rides. Similarly, your primal eating intelligence is used now to send you hunger only a few minutes before the main meal. And if you eat exactly as much as your eating intelligence requests during the main meal, then it will last you exactly until the following main meal, and you do not have to be bothered by hunger between meals ever again. And if you drink water at the end of each meal if necessary, you do not have to be bothered with thirst between meals either. And so you have your entire time to fulfill your higher human needs, since these are demanding.

Keeping the inner harmony is only a matter of being able to cooperate with your primal intelligences, since they are just as alive and capable as you are as a conscious intelligence. Even more, you only refer to yourself as being conscious because you are not capable to access directly the consciousness of your other intelligences in order to witness how conscious they are, since from their own perspectives, they are just as conscious as you are. And it is not a matter of inability not being able to access your other intelligences directly, since intelligences are unique and distinct. And therefore, you can never enter their mind directly at will, just as you cannot pass through people in the outside world. And if you can ever access intelligences directly to interconnect with them at least temporarily, as you do with your memories and senses of perception, then you consider these as part of yourself. Yet these are not primal intelligences, since they are significantly smaller, and they are designed to interact with you directly, as many of your motor intelligences do.

And again, you cannot understand your primal intelligences unless you understand yourself. As a reference, your primal intelligences are exactly the little kid that you once were when you were playing happily the entire time, because back then, your conscious intelligence was less developed, and therefore less capable to dominate them. While your primal intelligences were capable to interact with the outside environment through you. And you grew up, while now you tend to relate more to the conscious intelligence, you are wise, strong, and highly assertive, while your primal intelligences might still be the little kid that you once were. Even more, all primal intelligences are capable to transfer themselves wholly from one generation to another as they never die, and now you find your own primal intelligences in your kids and they might even look familiar, since they are pieces of you and you have to put up with them once again now, just as you have to tend to your cognitive system your entire life, and just as your parents had to put up with you when you grew up.

What happens with all intelligences of all cognitive systems is that they strive to gain and maintain individuality, unique specialization, and therefore unique identity. Because if you happen to have two similar intelligences and more within any cognitive system, then these are considered as one intelligence. And among all, the number of specializations available within any cognitive system, class system, organism, or in any living environment is limited, and this makes for a limited number of intelligences present in any cognitive system at a time. It is only when the outside environment changes, for various reasons, that the specific cognitive system has to expand its tasks, meanings, and specializations. And this is exactly how intelligences are born, taking all opportunities to occupy newer and newer living niches every time these appear. And it is a very strong competition for each new specialization formed in this manner. And this explains development and adaptation to any environment better than the theory of evolution and the survival of the fittest.

Yet you are highly privileged and highly recognized as a unique, pertinent conscious intelligence within your cognitive system and therefore within your organism. Who are you exactly? You have many selves, since you have one self for each one of your environments. You are the conscious intelligence within your cognitive system, but you are also your inner self within your inner replica of this world. While you are also the physical organism within the outside world. And you have many other selves in all your realities, inner and higher, since you live a multidimensional life even simultaneously, starting with your videogame characters from your computer worlds since these inhabit inner realities, and you cannot interact with these inner videogame environments but through your videogame characters. And in a very similar manner, your soul or souls have you here in this world, since they cannot interact with this world but through you, through your physical body.

And so on, you have one self in the minds of all those around, matching the exact understanding that they have of you from the outside world, and even from your inner worlds. And then, there are your dream selves from all your dream worlds, along with your higher selves from your higher worlds, along with your social selves from the multitude of your social environments. And in all these environments and realities, you have a unique meaning, you tend to fulfill it with your specific self from that specific environment, and you should always account for all these.

Let us study now your first three selves, your conscious intelligence, your inner self, and your physical body. Because you might live your entire life by assuming that these three separate selves are only one, and this leads to discrepancy and misunderstanding throughout life.

You as a conscious intelligence reside throughout the body, within many cellular membranes of your organism, since you are a cellular intelligence. Yet all intelligences are cellular intelligences and subcellular intelligences, forming systems of intelligences form there to reach and span the entire organism. While you the conscious intelligence, in order to reason intelligently, you have to avate in your intelligent inner self from the left prefrontal lobe of your cortex. You may even see yourself on the display of an EEG machine, just by engaging in conscious reasoning then, since you are always lighten up there every time you are conscious. That is really you there, a small dot, a light in the prefrontal cortex, always turned on when you are consciously active, and this is how you may see yourself. And from that small group of neurons, you may extend yourself through axons and dendrites, to reach your senses of perception areas throughout the cortex, to reach your limbs through motor neurons and walk around, or to reach cortex areas holding memories every time you need them throughout your reasoning.

All your primal intelligences may do the same, and many monitor continuously the outside world, for all details and circumstances favorable to their specialization. Your primal eating intelligence may search for food continuously, for rare nutrients and vitamins, and so you feel the need to eat that specific food just by seeing or smelling the food product. Or your security primal intelligence may take complete control of your body if it sees imminent signs of danger, suddenly engaging in running, jumping, screaming, or dodging on its own, without your conscious intervention, every time imminent dangers occur. And it does a good job keeping you alive so far.

And you should always monitor and identify the entire activity of your primal intelligences taking place in this manner, since this is the only manner in which you may become aware of the specific nutrients that your body needs, and therefore you should add them in the menu of your next meal. Otherwise, your primal eating intelligence will make you eat unnecessarily, and then attempt to construct from scratch the needed nutrient if it is not essential, and you might end up losing vitality, getting sick, or even losing or gaining weight. And this takes you out of homeostasis, as it certainly interferes with the fulfillment of your higher human needs, and therefore with the fulfillment of your meanings in life and in this world. While if you fail to do what your security primal intelligence demands from you every time it sends you fear or discomfort, then you end up suffering in consequence, just because your primal intelligences are capable to perceive by far more than you do in the outside world while they monitor the outside world through your senses of perception. While you should always cooperate and maintain the harmony, because you the conscious intelligence are not the cognitive system, you do not rule the cognitive system, you are not the strongest and the most pertinent intelligence in your cognitive system, and if you fail to cooperate with all intelligences of your cognitive system when they send you your needs and meanings, if you fail to identify, consider, and fulfill your needs and meanings exactly as you are demanded to do, you end up disabled, sick, misfortunate, and even dead.

As an intelligent inner self, you are also a cellular intelligence, in your prefrontal lobe of your cortex. One single neuron would suffice to hold you, if individual neurons would not die frequently. You need an entire group of neurons for their multitude of connections, while you also need to be able to shift from one neuron to another whenever these die. And if your entire group of neurons dies for any reason, for sickness or trauma, then you die too as an intelligent inner self, and this is it, life is over for you. Yet the entire organism still survives, because there are countless of intelligences ready to take your place. Not your primal subconscious intelligences, since these already have their own meanings and tasks throughout the organism, but smaller intelligences will emerge from adjacent areas in the prefrontal cortex where you once were, or coming even from your opposite prefrontal lobe, since you use that area as a conscious copilot.

Now as an organism, you have to live life with a brand new intelligent inner self, having different tastes, habits, identity, and personality. And now you have no identity memory at all, since all neural connections lead to the disabled area from the prefrontal cortex where you once lived, and it takes time now to change the plasticity of the brain. While all your subconscious primal intelligences are just fine, and if you know how to interact with them, they can help you fulfill their needs as much as they can remember.

And this is how you can remember everything that your primal intelligences can remember about the outside world, but you cannot remember what is more important for you, the identity part found at the core of your inner replica of this world, simply because you are not there anymore as an intelligent inner self, because you are dead.

Doctors will label you with total amnesia, while your loved ones have to get used to you, and to understand you better, since you are someone else now, a different living being, which happens to inherit an older brain and organism, and a newly configured cognitive system. But you are someone else, you are a new intelligent you.

It is relevant to know that all intelligences have to learn throughout life, in order to help them reason while fulfilling their needs, tasks, specializations, and meanings. As a conscious intelligence, you have to learn everything about the outside environment relevant to the fulfillment of your needs, all your needs, of all levels. You learn everything that you find relevant, and you try to remember it well, only not to have to reinvent the wheel every time you fulfill a need. While you receive countless of needs throughout the day and throughout life and you have to fulfill them, but first you have to know exactly how to fulfill them.

You may learn what to do throughout school, by watching TV, or by interacting online, or you may learn throughout all your experiences, throughout the fulfillment of the rest of your needs. And every time you learn, you do not simply dump data in some area of your middle cortex, you do not arrange this data nicely into rows and columns as books are arranged in a library, but you arrange all information that you learn and understand in the exact form and manner that you find it in the outside world, only to be able to retrieve it quickly and accurately whenever necessary. Because you do not remember your knowledge by using tables of addresses, as computers and libraries do, but you always access related subjects nearby your current subject of perception or interest, for additional information, for anything that you can remember about, anything that you may relate. And if that specific information is arranged in the inner world of your memories exactly as it is found in the real world, then it will certainly show up throughout your thinking, since it is already connected with your entire subject of interest.

And this how your inner replica of this world matches and superimposes accurately on the outside world while you perceive and study it, while you do not even realize it, considering everything to be the outside world, followed only by some random thoughts that you suddenly have throughout your specific enquiry about the outside world.

And this is exactly how you have ended up with an entire inner replica of the outside world, after a lifetime of learning. And you replicate there not only objects and concepts, but people, along with everything that you know and understand about them. And these memories are accurate, living intelligences, found now in your inner replica of this world, including your inner self, since throughout life, you replicate yourself there, within your inner world, placed always at its center. And as an inner self, you are a genuine, living, reasoning intelligence within your inner replica of this world, and there is where you live.

All intelligences of all cognitive systems construct in this manner their own inner replicas of this world through learning, replicas trying to match their outer environment as much as possible, in order to help them memorize the outside world, and in order to help them think and find various solutions to the multitude of their experiences and occurrences, while they are interacting and coping with their environment, and while they are fulfilling their needs and meanings throughout their life. Because all intelligences are conscious intelligences having the task to interact with their outside cognitive environment within their cognitive system, only that their own immediate outside world within their cognitive system happens to be specialized. And this is how you perceive them as specialized intelligences, having in this manner their own set of tasks, needs, and meanings.

There are many reasons for constructing an entire inner reality matching the outside environment, and memorization is not the main cognitive activity. All intelligences think and reason within their own replicas of their immediate environment. There is where they understand the outside environment by creating additional links among all information, and by creating mental models in any way possible. And this is exactly how intelligences reason as seen from the inside of the cognitive system, they simply make mental models predicting the future in this manner, or predicting a possible version of the future, by setting discrete scenes of their inner worlds and letting them play or enact in this manner freely, to see what results they get.

You do the same through your reasoning and daydreaming, since you also set specific conditions to your inner world and then you let it unfold freely, to see what happens. You are caught by all inner circumstances, it is amusing, while it helps you understand the outside world from all possible circumstances that you might never have the opportunity to experience in the outside world, for various reasons. And experience is the key to your learning, since the more you experience, the more you have the chance to learn and understand firsthand this world outside. And since you may experience only the things that you are allowed, then daydreaming and inner simulation of the outside world are the key for learning and developing.

Yet even daydreaming is not the main reason for having an entire inner world matching the outside world at your disposal. Because all mental models that you may create in your inner replica of this world allow you to experience this world as fast simulations, in your mind first, before everything happens in the outside world, rendering yourself prepared in this manner, and helping you find solutions to problems that might have not even occurred yet.

All living beings think and behave in this manner, only that animals use algorithmic and intuitive thinking. While humans may use these two forms of lower level thinking, along with accurate mental models and intelligent reasoning, which are two intelligent human cognitive activities.

I use these higher cognitive activities in order to construct my intelligent models throughout this book and throughout this entire book series. As a reference, beliefs can barely use algorithmic thinking, which is first level thinking, while animals use mostly intuitive thinking, which is a second level thinking. Intuitive thinking consists of very rudimentary mental models formed by very simple yet very fast stimulus-response memory reflexes, since intuitive thinking is capable to use memorized information, just because both the stimulus and response components have feelings embedded in them, good or bad. And now you know exactly what will happen if you use that specific procedure throughout the fulfillment of your need or meaning, because you know in advance how you will feel if you behave in that specific manner.

And you know it too as a human being, since humans have these simplistic intuitive memories in their inner replica of this world, and within the inner replicas of all primal specialized intelligences. And many times, this is how primal intelligences send you their needs, through their own simplistic understanding of that specific circumstance. You know it in this manner in advance, you know what happens next and you know how your reward or punishment will feel if you behave that way, you choose the best feeling and therefore the best procedure, and this is how you now behave, intuitively. Or this is the case if you live your life on lower developmental levels, when you drift around throughout life carried by your own instincts, while chasing your good feelings and while doing your best to avoid your pain.

And this world is full of people living life in this manner, instinctually and therefore superficially, with everything always happening to them and taking them by surprise. While psychology considers intuitive thinking to be the most evolved cognitive activity that you have, praising it. As science always tells you that you are nothing but an animal, living your life in an animal world, while the entire society is at an animal level, with everybody around and on TV behaving on animal levels and lower. While education teaches you throughout life everything that you need to know in order to live your life as an animal and lower, as these are elaborate methods used by the Consensual Matrix to keep you underdeveloped, weak, predictable, and therefore under control and exploited.

Because there are even lower developmental levels below the second, animal level, only that the zero and first developmental levels are both consensual, integral part of the Consensual Matrix. Therefore, if you happen to live your life on even lower developmental levels, at the first consensual level, in servitude, you cannot do anything without the approval of your master or ideology, both being part of the same matrix as you are. While if you live your life at the zero developmental level, you take drugs to feel good, and you take more drugs to avoid pain.

And for all these developmental levels, your inner replica of this world is distinct, just because your understanding of this world is very different at each level, and therefore its main structure is distinct for each level. And since your thinking is what you use in order to decide how to behave throughout life, you cannot actually choose your developmental level and therefore behavioral level throughout life, because you have to restructure and improve significantly your entire inner replica of this world in order to do so. While your inner replica of this world is a lifetime effort as it is, and it is very rigid, as it takes significant ability, persistence, and accuracy to be able to advance from lower developmental levels to higher ones. And now, if you try to compare what they do during AAA meetings with what it is actually required for you to advance from the zero developmental level to the actual human level, AAA seems more as a happy reunion.

Yet the inner replica of this world has other purposes besides memorization, simulating outside environments, predicting future outcomes through mental models, or finding solutions for all needs and meanings. The main reason for having an inner replica of the outside world is to have your own private environment, your own private world where you can live and subsist as well and as much as you please, if only in your mind, along with countless of beings as you. Because this is why intelligences construct these inner realities. Because all these inner replicas of the outside environments hold inner intelligences inside as seen from the outside world, while these inner intelligences are genuine objective living beings from the perspective of their inner reality, since they live in there just as their higher counterparts live in the outside world.

And this is how you think, perceive, memorize, reason, daydream, and mental model, through your inner replica of this world, but more importantly, you do so through the multitude of inner intelligences that you have there within your inner replica of this world, and they are actually the ones doing the modeling and simulations for you, as though it was all new and very real for them, probably not even knowing that they are only inner beings in an inner world, always performing throughout life as genuine actors on a stage.

And since there are zillions of intelligences in this world, inner, and higher, with each one creating their own inner worlds, filling them up with a zillion inner intelligences that also create their own inner inner worlds throughout thinking and learning, filling them up with inner inner intelligences, depending on what the current higher cognitive task demands, now they are filling up the entire wider world with zillions upon zillions of realities, all nested in each other in particular manners, with this world as only one of them, placed somewhere in a rime, as it is caught in a higher cognitive task. And this is exactly how the wider world has a cognitive meaning, and this is how you too have a cognitive meaning as seen from above, as seen from an upper perspective.

And now you know your meaning in this world and in the wider world, because you are part of an extraordinary cognitive activity of higher meaning along with everybody else, actors on a stage, play after play, dream after dream, and mental model after mental model. And now you know your meaning in the wider world, since the wider world is everything that exists, as everything is part of the Divine. And therefore, everything happening in the wider world and in all its realities has one meaning, to serve the Divine. And so you serve Life and the Divine, with each real, natural, living need and meaning that you fulfill, every moment of your life. And you are already fulfilling your higher meaning well, every moment of your life, through everything that you do and think normally, naturally. So make everything count, because life is never random, trivial, optional, or irrelevant, but it really counts, every moment, so make it a good one.

As you notice, your inner cognitive environment is not at all made of little electric snakes and worms, but it is filled with everything from the outside world, everything of interest at least, all found there in their exact shape, form, and arrangement as it is found in the outside world. While all significant intelligences from your inner replica of this world and from the rest of your cognitive system pressure you and send you needs continuously to give them news about their outside counterparts, along with everything happening in the outside world, all changes occurring out there, in order to be able to keep your inner replica of this world as synchronized as possible with the outside world, and to keep the inner characters of your inner world in continuous concordance with their outer counterparts.

This entire cognitive process of creation of an entire inner reality as a perfect replica of another outer reality may seem a trivial task now, but it is highly demanding, since it involves a high cognitive effort from the part of most of your cognitive system. And therefore, you should not underestimate it, but fulfill it accordingly, because as a conscious intelligence, this creation is one of your main meaning within your cognitive system.

As a reference of the complexity of this cognitive task, the entire brain expands in volume with the size of your replica of this world. When you study all species that have brain, from fish up, you may find a direct correspondence between the size of their group and the size of their brain. And this is the case just because the size of their brain corresponds to the size of their inner world, which is larger with an increased number of members of their group, herd, pack, or school, since the number of all members defines exactly the size of the actual social environment. And this is significant in our study, since your immediate society where you spend your life, besides your family, is your actual environment, accustoming you even for life. Larger cities can offer larger environments, while rural or remote, small, isolated communities shrink not only your actual environment and therefore lifestyle, but they shrink your inner replica of this world considerably, with significant consequences.

Yet animal inner replicas of this world are significantly different than human replicas of this world, since animals lack abstract reasoning and abstract understanding of this world as humans have, while humans lack direct connectivity among the multitude of distinct intelligences found in the other replicas of this world from the entire group, cognitive ability that humans refer to as telepathy. While this higher cognitive ability is different than what you find in science fiction today. These are the kind of cognitive abilities that the Consensual Matrix had managed to remove from your cognitive system, and this is how you have to live your life from now on, disconnected from the rest of this world. How exactly does it feel to live your life connected or disconnected from this world? It is about as it feels to live your life with Wi-Fi and cell signal, or without. But with drastic consequences.

And since you see the outside world through your inner replica of this world, you see and understand yourself from the outside world as your inner self, or through your inner self. And you are not your conscious intelligence as an inner self either, because you two reside in different places. And now you are together as one, because you are capable to maintain a direct neural link with your inner self as it is your avatar. You have managed to take over your inner self in this manner and it is a genuine case of possession, yet you were the one creating your inner self anyway. And this is how you live your life now, through your inner self, as your inner self, within your inner world.

Or this is the case when you reason or daydream, because you still have two different lives now, as your inner self within your intelligent inner replica of this world spanning the cortex, and as the physical body in the outside world. And you live your life in this manner in two separate environments even simultaneously, as two separate selves, the inner self, and the outer self or physical body, having two separate meanings and identities, one in the outside world, and one in your inner world.

To be more precise now, you are an entire lifeline of existence, with all selves on it, all living life one through another through another. Because you are soul, mind, and body as one, in this order, and on this specific lifeline of existence.

Yet there are more souls and inner selves on your lifeline of existence, since your souls have souls, avating one through another. You have three main inner selves, since you have three brains one on top of another. While the conscious intelligence has to avate through all three before it reaches the outside world as the physical body, in the outside world.

In short, if the conscious intelligence wants to reason, it does so as the intelligent inner self from the cortex. If it reads romance novels, it has to do so through the intuitive inner self from the middle reptilian brain. If it wants to interact in the outside world, then it has to avate once more as the intelligent inner self, and then again through it, it has to avate as the physical body in the outside world.

But in general, the conscious intelligence avates in all inner selves and then in the outside world, managing in this manner to reason continuously intuitively and intelligently, while interacting in the outside world. With all souls avating in the conscious intelligence continuously, and through it, being the intelligent inner self and or the physical body, interacting in the outside world. Yet at times, souls have their own higher lives in their higher worlds, and you do not know if they are with you or not. While other souls are with you in this world continuously, since they have their loved ones here.

While the entire time, for you the conscious intelligence, it makes little difference if the souls are here with you. Yet your comprehensive conscious cognition tends to become very complex and very fulfilling when you have all souls and all inner selves involved, while you and those around you can tell the difference. While throughout artistic circumstances, you have to have your souls involved, since art is the entertainment of the souls, as it is performed by the souls and for the souls. While if you become involved as a conscious intelligence or inner self, you end up with trash mostly, but not with art.

Yet not only the conscious intelligence and the inner selves create their own inner worlds where they learn and reason, but all primal intelligences of your cognitive system do, they construct their own inner replicas of this world in order to be able to learn and remember, so they do not have to reinvent the wheel every time they fulfill their specialized needs. Only that their replicas of this world are different, since they include only whatever is relevant to their specialization from the outside world and from inside the organism and cognitive system. There are the fridge and the grocery stores memorized by your eating primal intelligence in its own specialized inner replica of this world, along with the best procedures that it may apply to you in order to determine you to cook and eat the necessary nutrients, along with how to make you chew and how to swallow the food, as this is a rather complex movement. And then there are procedures of how to digest these throughout the stomach in the most efficient manner, how to store and distribute them, and how to use them throughout the trillions of cells. And this is the case with all your primal intelligences, since they have their own specialized inner replicas of this world throughout the main subconscious intelligence.

And now, we may be able to see how intelligences send you needs throughout life, since all do. Yet they do not send needs only to you the conscious intelligence, but they send needs to all primal intelligences of your cognitive system, subduing them, whenever needed, forming specific axis of hormones always present throughout the organism.

How do they do so? First, you have to understand that your primal intelligences do not reside in the brain, in some area of the cortex as you do, but they cover the entire organism, according to their specific task within the organism. Your primal eating intelligence resides in the stomach almost entirely, while also having access to all the cells of the body as it sends to them nutrients, and while storing in some of them part of these nutrients.

Even more, physical bodies do not actually hold intelligences and the entire cognitive systems as cups hold water, but they hold them within entire inner worlds or inner realities. And everything seems real, objective, and material within any reality, inner or outer, as long as you are there. This is why you never realize that you are dreaming while you are within your dream realities, because everything is real and objective there, as long as you remain there. Therefore, while for you, reasoning may seem immaterial and abstract as you notice it from the perspective of the outside world, this reasoning is done by the inner intelligences of the conscious intelligence, in an objective manner from their own perspective, and they do so just by moving around naturally for any reason, or just by interacting and communicating naturally with relevant intelligences there within your inner replica of this world or anywhere within your cognitive system, in an objective, material manner. You also reason through mental models, with inner intelligences interacting objectively, normally, within inner replicas of this world, not even knowing that everything is only a simulation, all happening in a mind, for cognitive purposes.

And this is how intelligences send needs, by acting directly on specific areas of the brain while meeting with other intelligences, or with you the conscious intelligence, in order to trigger specific feelings while they inform you directly of what the problem is, so you may know in advance what everything is and how you will feel if you do or do not fulfill their needs. Since you have been there before, and you know the need.

Or this is the case if you live your life at the second, animal level, because at the intelligent human level, you can simply feel your primal intelligences and therefore you know everything happening within your mind and body. And many times, you are already prepared to receive your need, and you may have it already covered.

And if you are very developed, then you may communicate normally with your primal intelligences. And if you still had your higher cognitive abilities, then you could communicate in a similar manner with all intelligences, not only with those of your cognitive system, but with those of all people and animals found everywhere. Since all animals communicate in this manner, because it is a natural cognitive ability. Just study your pets, and try to distinguish them talk to each other when they are excited, because they can get loud then. And if they identify you, they might even talk with you. Or this is the case if they do not have additives in their food, because these are meant to remove higher abilities.

How do intelligences send their needs? Do they simply push big red buttons on the brain, one for pleasure, another one for pain and discomfort, and another one for love? Yes, this is how they do so, only that they do not actually push buttons, but they interact directly in particular manners within the specific area where you reside, within your specific cognitive environment. What intelligences do in order to travel throughout the organism, they form overall cellular membranes through specific ions that they place between cells and at the synapses if they use neurons throughout connections, and this is how they unite their own cellular membrane where they reside with any cellular membrane where they need to go, forming in this manner a large, overall world that they may span freely to interact with any intelligence found there, or even with you the conscious intelligence, for as long as they need. And since time is different in other realities than what you experience here in our world, it might take but a fraction of a second for intelligences to interact, and then they disconnect the overall cellular membrane. You may see this cognitive process on an EEG display, since the entire overall ionic membrane lights up while connected and while intelligences move around. And it is very fast, with a multitude of similar overall interconnectivities occurring each second, depending on needs and circumstances. And then, when intelligences interact, they use and manipulate knowledge, thoughts, and feelings, just as you carry and manipulate material objects here in our world. Because feelings and thoughts as you experience them from the perspective of this world in a subjective manner are objective in nature within the inner realities where they occur. Because existence has three natures: subjective, objective, and highjective, and these are only relative existential perspectives following the existential relationship that realities have among themselves. Therefore, as seen from the inner, cognitive perspective, everything is done materially and objectively, as it seems to be more as physical constraints or harassment, or as physical gratification, depending on the feeling, if it is punishment or reward.

In order to understand exactly how it is done, you have to understand how all primal intelligences exist. Many primal intelligences do not exist as entire cellular intelligences, but depending on when they had appeared throughout the development of organic life, these primal intelligences are now still in the exact form that they were when they first appeared. Well, they are not only in this same form and shape, but they are the exact beings that they were then, long ago, and throughout the entire development of organic life. Because intelligences live directly in the field, and they only transfer themselves from one physical body to another, which are also made of the field.

Intelligences are capable to unite their inner worlds sometimes, if needed, in order to form extraordinary overall realities comprising tens of millions of cells, if only instantaneously. While the multitude of intelligences interacting throughout any inner reality, larger or smaller, always remain distinct and unique. But they do not actually unite themselves in order to form larger intelligences, but they may only live their lives in communities, forming in this manner larger and larger cognitive systems as needed, where they specialize just as cells do throughout organisms and as people do throughout societies.

And this is not only a comparison with cells and people, because the specific intelligences found within cells and people allowing them to specialize are the exact ones found in cognitive systems, since it is only a matter of perspective, to see individuals of all classes as physical bodies, or as living beings, or as intelligent beings. They are the same lifeline of existence either way, and it is only a matter of choice if you want to perceive them as physical organisms formed of cells and cellular components, or as an entire cognitive system formed of primal intelligences that are formed of inner intelligences that are formed of inner inner intelligences. Yet all these intelligences, at all levels of existence, are simply communities of intelligences, and not amalgamations of smaller intelligences melted in one, because all intelligences keep their uniqueness, identity, specialization, lifeline, and individuality in all cognitive systems.

And it is the same with the cells of your organism, since when you study them closely, you find them only floating in ions or plasma one near another, but not actually touching each other, since cells are also alive, individual, and unique, as they keep their own specialization within the organism. And it is the same with people within societies, with sheep on pastures, and with ants underground, since they keep their uniqueness, identity, individuality, and specialization within their groups and communities. This is significant to understand, since it will help us understand your meaning in life and in this world, and who or what exactly gives you your meaning in life and in this world.

Together, bodies and intelligences define life. And these are the perspectives of the Divine or the One: Life, Intelligence, Interconnectivity, and the wider world, as they are the perspectives of any living being, of any lifeline, at their own level, since everything and everyone exists, is alive, and is intelligent, as the same Existence defines them, in various forms of life and throughout all realities. It only happens that Biology studies only organic life, and even so, it studies it only within this world. While as you notice, there is more to consider about life, intelligence, and this world.

And it is not a coincidence that both intelligences and physical bodies are made of the field and exist in the field, which is the well-known electromagnetic field that you may identify here at a macroscopic scale. Because you cannot actually tell apart intelligences from their physical bodies, when you study them at their own scale, inner or outer, depending on the class of life that you study. This is the case with all your cells and cellular components, since at microscopic and nanoscopic scales, you cannot perceive material details anymore, but only variations in the field displacement, along with the continuous, comprehensive interaction within the field. And this is why you have to add ink in order to see cells and cellular components, while what you see is not exactly the material cell along with its components, but it is the pigment of the ink, as it takes the shape of the field throughout the cell.

Even light has no meaning to consider at nanoscopic scales, since its wavelength exceeds the scale of your subject of study. Electronic microscopes are another example, since through them, you see nothing material as they display, but you see various distributions of the field along with all interaction taking place within the field distribution, just because electrons are simply field distribution, not even elementary particles. And even so, even at nanoscopic levels, you are still capable to see how physical bodies hold their intelligences within their inner realities, while these are made by the same field, to the point that you cannot distinguish one from the other. Because physical bodies are made of field directly, but their inner realities and intelligences are made and held through specific, coded interactions happening within the field, while inner realities and the intelligences are not held directly by the field, but by these encoded interactions of the field distribution itself. While these coded interactions are made possible by the bodies holding their intelligences as they interact with the field, in an intelligent coded manner.

Yet these are simplistic models of elemental ionic living beings made of one simple body and one elemental intelligence, while the multitude of intelligences living in one cell or neuron live within composites of bodies formed by a multitude of distinct vibrating molecules, which form together larger molecules, as proteins or steroids. And even so, these hold larger, overall systems of intelligences held within entire groups and arrays, and these are larger and highly pertinent intelligences as seen from above, yet they are still composed of distinct individual inner intelligences as seen from within. You are one of them as you reside somewhere within your own small group of neurons in the cortex, while your primal intelligences are capable to span the organism, and they may even exit your body in order to enter other organisms, of all those around, through the same arrays of ions, proteins, and steroids, many times through the same arrays holding them within your organism.

And even so, this is how you may see your intelligences

here in this world through their physical bodies, because they actually live within the inner realities of your cognitive system. And there they live in a normal, casual, material, objective manner, alongside a multitude of other relevant, specialized intelligences, just as we live among other people here in our world.

I only refer to them as intelligences, since they make the subject of this study, yet when you consider them along with the physical bodies holding them, they are genuine living beings and should be considered accordingly. Because life exists at all class levels, and therefore cellular components are alive just as cells are alive, organisms are alive, communities, civilizations, and entire realities are alive. Even more, you can never find anything that is void of life, because life is present everywhere, in all forms of life, molecular, cellular, organic, plasmatic, ionic, and crystalline.

Many intelligences are in the same form and shape as they were even before organic life, when they were of the ionic form of life or molecular form of life, as ions, amino acids, proteins, steroids, and RNAs. And now, you may see easily all primal intelligences at work throughout the body in form of subcellular intelligences as simple ions, amino acids, proteins, and steroids. And as stated above, primal intelligences are capable to exit cells and span the entire organism, as arrays of their own material and ionic components, as arrays of ions, amino acids, proteins, and steroids as you find them throughout the endocrine and exocrine systems. This is the order of development, with the eating primal intelligence to be among the oldest ones, and with the reproductive intelligence among the newest ones, now using arrays of steroids. Steroids are more developed cellular components, using fatty acids within their structure, and therefore surpassing proteins. Medicine refers to all primal intelligences as hormones or neurotransmitters, since this is how it sees them here in this world. Yet medicine and science never research other realities, inner or outer, and they are never capable to understand hormones and neurotransmitters as the overall inner intelligences that they carry, but only as physical bodies. Because all cognitive systems and therefore all intelligences are held within inner realities, just as computer hardware holds the software within inner, digital realities.

And in order to send you needs now, your primal intelligences have to constrain you or favor you within your own cognitive environment, and you feel it either as good or bad feelings. It is this specific feeling that you receive, as a taste of what it is to come if you only fulfill the need, or if you fail to fulfill it. Yet you already know what you have to do, since you have felt hunger many times throughout life, and you already know that you have to eat and what you have to eat, in what amount. You also know all consequences if you do not eat, since you have been there before, and so you act accordingly. And that was your need, with many more to come.

There is more to consider, because the Consensual Matrix indoctrinates you not to eat, or to eat harmful food, or to eat toxic food additives. These harm your entire body and cognitive system, yet you need the nutrients so you still have to eat the additives, it darkens your cognitive system and nothing works as it should, the inner harmony is broken many times, you are blocked and you cannot communicate directly with your primal intelligences, and you lose connectivity with other cognitive systems. And there is nothing that you can do as a conscious intelligence. Many organisms even get sick and die because of these chemical additives, and there is nothing that you can do even as a primal eating intelligence. Because the Consensual Matrix has your body and mind, both on physical and cognitive levels.

What is relevant to notice here is how your primal intelligences actually live and behave within your cognitive system, since they do so just as normally and just as casually as normal people do in this world. Only that they have their own specialized environments, as they look significantly different than regular humans. In fact, your primal intelligences are mastodons in your cognitive world, being composed by smaller and smaller intelligences down to the slightest subcellular intelligences of your physical body.

While everything resembles life here in the real world, since you as a physical body are composed of trillions of cells yourself, which are composed of zillions of cellular components, down to the slightest intelligences of the field. I refer to these as classes of life, since life tends to gather into larger and larger systems of life: ions, molecules, cells, organisms, communities, societies, species, civilizations, and realities. Life is everywhere, on all levels, in all classes, in all forms, and in all realities, since everything is alive and intelligent. And everywhere you are, either as a cell, cellular component, organism, or society, you have your own surrounding outer environment, while you have your own reasoning and memories to form your inner environment, which is your inner replica of this world, helping you reason and fulfill your needs in the outer environment. Since you always receive needs, and you have to fulfill them.

As a conscious intelligence, throughout life, you always interact with your outside environment in order to fulfill your needs, while you alter your outside environment simultaneously in order to facilitate the fulfillment of your own needs, also altering it in this manner in order to facilitate the fulfillment of the needs of all those around. Because this is exactly why Life folds upon herself, in order to form higher and higher forms of life and classes of life, as cells, organisms, communities, and worlds, only in order to have individual living beings working together toward the fulfillment of all their needs, since all their needs are similar in nature. As it is by far easier and more efficient to have them fulfilled synchronously, in a specialized, well-defined manner, so they never have to work one against another while fulfilling their needs.

And this is exactly how specializations or meanings are formed, as part of entire communities and societies. Since this is how meanings appear, constituting everything that you do for your environment, being it natural, social, inner, higher, cognitive, or informational.

And what if you refuse or are incapable to fulfill your meaning or specialization for your natural or social environment, for your family, nation, or community? Is there Life herself standing near you with a little notebook to record everything that you ever do for all your environments including for her? No, not at all, since you are already part of Life, as an intelligent living human being. Even more, your own intelligences are more faithful to Life herself, than they are to you the living human being. With your needs and meanings already embedded in your inner cognitive environment, in your cognitive system, already coming from your primal intelligences, and you have to fulfill them eventually, since this is how you are constrained. Because throughout normal, living, successful environments, it is never a matter of will, if you want or not to fulfill your needs and meanings, but it is a matter of capability and success, if you are capable to fulfill them or not.

Because naturally, you already have your punishment-reward cognitive mechanism rewarding and constraining you to fulfill your needs and meanings, and you know exactly what to do. And this is what you always do. While your own intelligences send you your needs and meanings in very large numbers because they have been doing so for generations, for entire civilizations, for entire species, and for entire forms of life, in order for you to tend to your organism, family, society, and entire inner and outer environments, exactly as they already know that it is the best for them, for you, for everyone else, and for Life herself.

More precisely, your intelligences know exactly what it is the best for you and for the entire outside world, since they have been there before, throughout the past ages of Earth and eons of existence, and now they choose the best of the best to have in this world, the golden ages of their previous lives and experiences. Which are the best of the best genuine human environments ever and more, since your intelligences always develop everything continuously, and now they make everything better. If you are only willing to fulfill your needs and meanings exactly as they send you the feelings.

While as you study closely all these, you notice how by neglecting, opposing, altering, or interfering with the needs, feelings, and meanings coming from your intelligences and from all intelligences of all living human beings, is as interfering with Nature herself, with this entire living world, with Mother Earth, with our own Creator, with Life herself, with the Deity, and with the entire wider world.

While the Consensual Matrix and all its slaves always interfere with all these, including with your own intelligences, their fulfillment, and with your entire meaning in life and in the world. And since these slaves form entirely the current consensual Brotherhood, invisible kingdom, dictators of the East and all their servants and slaves, and the entire Elite, you stand no chance.

Yet when you study these servants and slaves even closely, you notice how they are all the humans in the world. And now you really stand no chance to fulfill your actual third level intelligent human needs and meanings in life and in the world, since you are the consensual world.

Your intelligences send you your needs in order for you to tend to them and to your entire organism as you interact as an entire organism in the outside world. But as you notice throughout this book, your intelligences also send you your meanings, to tend to the entire outside world, where you fulfill your needs, in order to have the outside world exactly as your intelligences desire. Because your own intelligences tend to you and to the entire outside world, in all its family, social, and environmental details. Because your needs tend to you, while your meanings tend to the entire outer environment, the entire family, the entire community, the entire living intelligent human society, and the entire real outside human world.

Since your intelligences know exactly what they want, as they have been in person throughout entire successful golden ages in the distant past, as human beings and other successful intelligent species before, and now they know exactly what to ask for. With Atlantis itself their most current successful golden human age, and with similar ones before. And you feel it too, as you call it care. A continuous care for the entire world, since this is why you feel bad every time you watch dreadful news on TV from the entire world. Or this is why you seek to help others with all their needs, since this is what meanings are, tending to the needs of others.

While as you study your intelligences and the entire outside world, your intelligences desire from you to change the outside world in the exact manner that they had it before in its most meaningful, most fulfilling, and most harmonious manner that it had ever been, and better. Since your intelligences, all living beings, and the entire Life always develop, always improve, always have everything better.

But this remains the case only if you fulfill your needs and meanings in the best, most successful, most meaningful, most fulfilling, and most harmonious manner. Because if you do not, if you are not successful, if you are only partially successful, or if you are not willing at all to fulfill your needs and meanings, Life takes you out, and it is game over.

Because death is not the opposite of Life as you are made to believe, since there is nothing opposing Life, as Life is everywhere and cannot be opposed. Death is not the end of Life either, since Life is eternal and cannot end. But death is an invention, ability, tendency, characteristic, or supreme law of Life, meant to take out everyone meaningless, unsuccessful, non-developing, old, unfulfilling, irrelevant, idle, and corrupt.

Since if you refuse to fulfill your meanings, you ruin everything in this world, while changing entire golden human ages into dark ages, and this is what you now have.

Because you do not listen to your feelings, needs, and meanings exactly as they come. And you do so not naturally, but you do so because you are constrained in other manners, through other forces, social and consensual, and this is what you always obey. Since this is exactly how your normal, genuine human meanings are altered in this world, changing an entire world, from human to consensual, enhancing servitude, instead of meaning. Since this is how you have the human servitude today, in an entire exploitive world, instead of the human meaning, in an entire meaningful, living, fulfilling, intelligent, harmonious world. And it is a significant difference.

Because some people, or many people have learned to tap into your feelings and meanings in order to exploit you and abuse you and your loved ones, in an organized manner, and now this is what they do, and what you do. This is basic organized crime, taking place at a universal scale, and since it has its own laws stating that it is legal and even mandatory for you to be exploited and to exploit others, now this is what you do along, with the entire world. And this is the Consensual Matrix. While the Consensual Matrix always interferes with your inner cognitive environment, family environment, and genuine human environment, to the point where your inner environment is already altered and decayed, while the genuine human environment is already lost and extinct, with only the Consensual Matrix in place, replacing it entirely. And with the Consensual Matrix reaching your family through all legal laws and constraints altering it, while reaching your inner cognitive environment through all its beliefs, stereotypes, and entire ideological dogma and juridical codes of law.

Yet consensus means agreement, and you always want to live in agreement, not in chaos and disagreement. Since this is the case in all nations of this world, because when you study this world closely, you notice how all dictatorships hide behind names as democracy, socialism, liberty, communism, equality, national, for the people, and prosperity, but they are always dictatorships. And it is the same with the entire Consensual Matrix, as it remains contorted by all tyrants and dictators, covertly in the West, and in the open in the East. Only that the Consensual Matrix is larger, covering most of the wider world, throughout zillions of worlds and realities, to do the same everywhere, while contorting everything, to have only dynasties, dictatorships, and tyranny everywhere, hidden or in the open.

Because when you have consensual environments as the Consensual Matrix, interfering with your natural environments, you fail to tend to your meaning or specialization, the entire environment suffers, it happens to everybody, nobody is capable anymore to tend to the world, and this is it, life is over.

Because this is what the Consensual Matrix does throughout worlds and civilizations, it keeps you away from tending to your natural meaning. And if you happen to be at the heart of your environment and you fail, then the entire environment has to die, just for you. And there are many cases in this world and throughout the history when entire nations fell, because the leader or ruler failed, or because their most important infrastructure fell, or because the borders failed, or because material and food supply failed to come in.

You might not be the ruler of an entire nation, but you are probably responsible with your family, or with an entire group of people at work, or you are responsible with your pets and plants, and by now, you know exactly how to tend to them, how to fulfill your meaning for them, and how to help them to fulfill their own meaning in their specific environment.

Responsibility is the key to understanding meanings within all environments, since not only humans have to fulfill their meanings, but animals do, and they do a good job, as all intelligences of all cognitive systems and all cells of all organisms do. Just study your own cells now, to see how they fulfill their meanings flawlessly and harmoniously, making your entire body be, look, and feel excellent. What happens when one cell decides to take a day off? It is marked at once as disabled, and it is recycled even from the inside out, making room for another cell to take its place. Because while your needs may depend on you and on your behavior, since needs come from the inside of your cognitive system, your meanings are the other way around, coming from your environment. Or this is the case apparently, because meanings come from intelligences, just as all needs do.

Your meanings address your environment or your higher class of life, and therefore they are addressed outside yourself, not affecting you directly, but affecting your entire environment, along with everybody comprising the environment. Because your meanings become a source or niche for others to fulfill their needs, through them, through you, through your meanings. Making an entire outside world possible, in a meaningful, harmonious, living manner. And this is what intelligences want, yours and theirs.

And it is the same with all primal intelligences, since they have their specializations within the organism, through similar specialized needs and meanings. And when one of them fails, then everyone fails. The entire body suffers consequently, so everybody makes sure that it never happens again.

Besides, as already seen, primal intelligences do not die, but they are transferred from one generation to another at the moment of conception, almost wholly. Because they are not exactly individual intelligences in themselves, but communities of intelligences, which can be separated and displaced with ease. They transfer themselves to the new generation in this manner, just as civilizations send colonies to new worlds. Because all intelligences are systems of intelligences themselves, or cognitive systems themselves. And this is how they reproduce, by sending colonies toward the new generations, becoming the new generations themselves. All primal intelligences do so, they interconnect with colonies sent by the other parent. And this is how children are formed, first within the egg, and the egg develops from then on to form the child, the latest member of the genetic line.

And this is how you live your life now. But who exactly is the living being? You? Your cells? The organism as a whole? The entire genetic line? The entire species? Because it seems that primal intelligences live life more as entire genetic lines, as entire species, and even as entire forms of life, since they have been around for a very long time. Which is an achievement. But now, if your eating primal intelligence fails, then the entire organism is affected, no one is fed, germs conquer, you get sick, and you may even die before you get to eat again. And it truly makes a difference when you have extra fat deposited within your body, just to make it through during the harsh diet. Because this is what the primal eating intelligence seeks.

Your primal reproductive intelligence is also significant to consider, yet this world certainly does not die if you are not too successful while on a date. It would be such a loss and a terrible disappointment not to score, but there are other weekends to come, other partners to have fun with, and life goes on. However, the need to engage in sexual activities is not the only need that your reproductive intelligence sends you, and you should be aware of them. Even more, this world does die if you do not score, because this might be your only chance to reproduce before time passes, since you grow old, and no one accepts you anymore as a favorable partner.

And this is the case not because this world runs out of favorable people to reproduce with, but because society is more austere in everything concerning reproduction. While having sex is a relatively straightforward activity, society makes so many rules, regulations, and restrictions concerning reproduction, that many people give up altogether. And even if you have a spouse, then you limit yourself to one or two children, if you ever want them, killing the rest even by the dozens. Is this what Life wants? No, since Life wants life, while the Consensual Matrix wants only the genetic lines of those ruling the Consensual Matrix to span this world and take it as their own, with you and your kind exterminated in the process. Unless you are a tyrant or dictator yourself.

How can the Consensual Matrix do this, while the need for reproduction is very persisting? The Consensual Matrix uses these specific rules and regulations in order to limit and even remove the act of normal, successful sexual interaction. Why don't people revolt at once for losing their chance to propagate their own genetic lines? The people themselves are the ones imposing all these measures to themselves, since this is how indoctrination works in all domains. If anyone tells you now that there should be no age regulation in everything involving reproduction as long as Life makes it possible to reproduce at that specific age, you will do everything to imprison them for what they say and do. Or you will accept it eventually, if everyone does, but you let it apply only to others, not to you and your family, because you are still in your right mind, and will always do as your doctrine tells you. And this is how those around have fewer restrictions now and they still manage to reproduce, while your own genetic line dies away.

But you have kept your doctrine and that might count, who knows. Yet this is not what happens in real life, because when the Consensual Matrix wants something, anything, even the extermination of entire worlds, then that is exactly what the Consensual Matrix has, just by making entire worlds to exterminate themselves, through the right doctrine. And this is how entire nations form Asia once famous for being able to reproduce prosperously, well known for their remarkable diverse genetic background, now, after the Consensual Matrix, they are the largest nursery homes for the old, soon to perish slowly, while keeping all their regulations involving reproduction instated with pride the entire time.

What exactly is your meaning in life in what it concerns reproduction? This is only your meaning within your genetic line, to keep it abundant and diverse, and you may do so by having children with a multitude of distinct partners.

And you will not overpopulate this world, since reproductive needs are second level needs, as eating, socializing, breathing, security, and recovery. And while fulfilling these, you always make sure that you do not harm those around. Because you never fulfill any need if your behavior harms those around. And this is how you never eat the doughnuts carried by strangers, but you eat your own food. You never drink the water of those who are thirstier than you, you do not harm others while trying to save yourself and your family during wars and calamities, but you even help those in need. Because overpopulation is only a myth, a common slogan found in all ideologies of the Consensual Matrix, meant only to allow the few powerful genetic lines found at the top of this world to reproduce as much as possible. And now, by using incubation technology at its best, these really multiply as much as possible, while you and your genetic line go extinct, since you are of a different kind and you stand in the way.

Since the Consensual Matrix makes it possible.

You certainly overpopulate this world in this offensive manner, if you are still on lower developmental levels, because at the intelligent human level, you make sure that you do not overpopulate this world excessively with your own genes. Yet study this case minutely now, to see how you never have to have two children or less in order to keep your genetic line steady, but you have to aim for five or six children in average. Otherwise, your genetic line shrinks, just because the Consensual Matrix indoctrinates everybody not to have children but to engage only in unsuccessful sexual interaction, for pleasure. Therefore, it is more likely that your children will not have children themselves, and so you have to have more children yourself, and so do your children and everybody else caught under the indoctrination of the Consensual Matrix. And if you have more children, then medicine targets you with terminal illnesses, and your genetic line still goes extinct. And now you have to dodge most of the current consensual society only not to go extinct.

Yet can you have and raise six children today? No, not unless you are rich and powerful. While the specific genetic lines of the rich and powerful of this world are the ones surviving in the Consensual Matrix anyway, with yours exterminated shortly. And do not expect to survive just because you are in the Brotherhood, or in the invisible kingdom, or a tyrant of the East, because you are exterminated, right after you exterminate those below. Since the Elite never does a thing, but only keeps this world. While reproducing massively and having a normal, abundant, very prosperous life.

As stated above, your need for sexual interaction is not the only need that your primal reproductive intelligence sends you. And it happens that all primal intelligences send you every need required for them to fulfill their meaning within your cognitive system, within your organism, within your genetic line, within society, within the human species, within the organic life, within this world, and higher above, in the higher worlds. Since all your primal intelligences have their meanings in all these environments and classes of life, just as you do as a conscious intelligence and as a physical body. And the same primal reproduction intelligence takes care not only of the actual sexual interaction, but of the egg, of its formation and development, of the fulfillment of all their needs, of their training, development, and education, and of everything involved in bringing human beings to life and in raising them to adult age, when they are capable to take care of themselves and of the entire genetic line, community, nation, and society. And this is why all needs related to your children come from your reproductive intelligence, and therefore they are related. Yet you are the one restricting your children's reproductive interaction instead of allowing them to train at times toward normal, successful interactions. Your genetic line suffers accordingly, your own reproductive intelligence punishes you accordingly for interfering with its meaning in life, yet the Consensual Matrix has you so indoctrinated, that you are ready to destroy countless of people and families only to keep your principles exactly as the Consensual Matrix requires. And you succeed in destroying these people, since all ideologies back you up, and consequently, your children will never have children anymore, since they find it to be such a hassle anyway. But they still live and die according to the Consensual Matrix and to all its laws, rules, and ideologies, childless.

How exactly does your reproductive intelligence know how to interact and with whom from the outside world? It happens that it knows more than you do about everybody from the outside world, in all details and from all perspectives. You might be able to notice bodily shapes and personality traces in order to help you with your decision in everything concerning your reproductive partners, while you always aim for an unsuccessful, non-productive interaction, killing yourself. While your reproductive intelligence knows everything about the genes and possibilities that your children have with those genes throughout life, and keeps sending you reproductive needs, always hoping to save you.

Because as stated, your primal intelligences do not die with the death of your physical body, but they are already within the next generations when your physical body dies. It is the same with you the conscious intelligence, since you are also a primal intelligence, and therefore you are already within the next generations whenever your physical body dies, in the exact form that you were at conception, as the small group of neurons from the left prefrontal cortex. It is you there in the next generation, along with parts of the conscious intelligence coming from the other parent. And it might be the primal reproductive intelligence deciding what goes to the next generation and what is discarded, as this is exactly why primal reproductive intelligences are interested in successful genes more than anything else. And what they do, they constrain you in every manner to meet that partner right away, and engage in sexual interactions at once. While your reproductive intelligence even enters the body of your perspective partner through pheromones, to determine him or her to accept you unconditionally. And this is what they should do, since they have always done so in the past throughout your entire genetic line, ever since the flat worms. While all your ancestors were highly successful, because if they were not, you were not here to tell the story. And if it was not for the Consensual Matrix with its strict rules, you already had your own children, and life went on.

The subject of reproduction is an important matter, and there is no reason to be restricted in any way through moral, legal, and ideological codes, rules, and principles, just because no one should ever interfere with the life of your perspective children. What exactly is wrong with reproduction? Why is reproduction considered repugnant and shameful in this world, while the entire world in all its species, classes, and forms of life reproduces successfully today, otherwise no one was here to tell the story?

How exactly do forms of life reproduce? Which exactly is the smallest form of life from the beginning? There is life at subatomic and sub-nuclear levels to consider, all the way down to the field itself, which is the Universal Mind. Intelligences originate in the field, and even when they manifest several forms of life above, as primal intelligences do, they are still anchored in the field. And now they reach upwards from there all the way to your level, and higher.

The lowest class level for the organic form of life is the molecule, or the cellular component. Cells are alive, they divide, and this is how they reproduce. You are actually a cell yourself, you are the original egg formed at conception, only that this egg had divided continuously, developing in this manner into this specific organism that you are today. However, you are still one cell, one cellular intelligence, since your organism is formed by the continuous division and development of one single cell. And this is the case for all upper classes of life, since they are formed as the continuous development of one organism, into an entire higher class of life, as the social class of life. It is the same with species, communities, and civilizations, since they have their origins in all lower classes of life and forms of life. Similarly, the entire organic form of life is based on the cellular form of life, molecular form of life, and ionic and plasmatic forms of life at its base, standing directly on top of these, as it had only become organic with the formation of organisms.

Yet there was life even before organisms and cells, living as communities of proteins, amino acids, ions, and RNAs, with your own primal intelligences being still alive then in these exact forms. Which were living their lives in water environments, without cellular membranes, as living arrays of ions, amino acids, proteins, and RNAs. And now, many times, some of your primal intelligences are capable to climb to the top of your cognitive system to send their needs and orders from there to the entire organism.

While we also notice how all intelligences are specialized, continuously fulfilling their own meanings in life and in their worlds and communities through these specializations.

Furthermore, since intelligences do not die, these specialized intelligences transcend from ions to molecules to cells and to organisms while fulfilling the same specialized meanings in all these forms of life. And these are your own primal intelligences of the entire organism, in their ionic and molecular forms as they have always been, only in larger systems of intelligences now, uniting to cover the entire cell and then the entire organism.

And this is the case because the field or Universal Mind holding intelligences is strong enough only at ionic and molecular scales, and therefore only at subcellular scales. Since organisms are too large to form their own intelligences, and so they have to sit on top of the previous forms of life, the ionic form of life, molecular form of life, and cellular form of life. With all these intelligences uniting in larger and larger systems of intelligences, covering the entire organism, as there are always the small inner ionic and molecular intelligences composing them.

To be more precise now, the organic form of life includes all life that lives as organisms. Yet the organic form of life stands on top of the cellular form of life. Since all cells are alive, and through their own life, they give life to the entire organism. Because you do not have the specialized cell in life, but all cells are similarly alive. Furthermore, when you study cells, you notice it composed of billions of cellular components, all alive and intelligent. Since all cellular components give life to the entire cell, because again, you do not have the molecule of life. And this is the molecular form of life, comprising all proteins, amino acids, RNAs, enzymes, steroids, DNA, and microtubules. Furthermore, ions themselves are alive and intelligent, at a smaller existential level, yet still forming an entire form of life, the ionic form of life.

Therefore, the molecular form of life stands on top of the ionic form of life. The cellular form of life stands on top of the molecular form of life. The organic form of life stands on top of the cellular form of life. While there is life above, and you may refer to it as upper forms of life or upper classes of life, since it is the same. As the social class of life, community class of life, national class of life, Mother Earth, and Life herself.

All classes of life above the organic form of life were

supposed to be alive, as the intelligent human society, or the intelligent human environment, if people were allowed to fulfill their actual human meaning in life and in this world. But the Consensual Matrix stops them, in order to make possible all these tyrants and dictators throughout the upper social layers of society, and now the human society is dead, consensually dead, killing all upper classes of life.

Yet forms of life and classes of life are only physical and social perspectives of intelligences, systems of intelligences, and entire cognitive systems. Because from a physical perspective, you see forms of life and classes of life. While from inner, subjective, cognitive perspectives, you see intelligences and systems of intelligences.

With Life herself becoming larger in size throughout all her forms of life, classes of life, and entire living worlds and realities, and becoming more capable cognitively through her larger and larger systems of intelligences. Because this is why you have forms of life on top of forms of life, in order to be able to form larger and larger systems of intelligences.

While the larger the system of intelligences is, the more capable it becomes, with more abilities and specializations included. Yet many times, systems of intelligences merge and divide temporarily, according to needs, modes, hierarchies, and specializations. Because as stated, all intelligences are systems of intelligences, while all systems of intelligences are societies or civilizations of living beings, but not exactly individual living beings. While you never have one body for one intelligence, but you always have one body for one system of intelligences, cognitive system, or entire civilization of intelligences. While at times, you have an entire array of similar bodies for one single system of intelligences.

And this is how you have the slightest specialized ionic intelligence. After uniting with all ionic intelligences in the area, it becomes similarly specialized now, but tending to an entire molecule. And with molecular specialized systems of intelligences uniting now within cells and entire organisms, you have the same little ionic specialized intelligence leading the rest, to tend to the entire cell, furthermore to tend to the entire tissue, organ, or bodily system, as an actual primal subconscious intelligence. While it is always the small ionic intelligence as it had always been. As it becomes in this manner through its own talent, uniqueness, success, and capabilities overtaking the rest. One in a zillion. Which is the case with you too as a conscious intelligence, since you have your roots in the raw field or Universal Mind just as well, as a small ionic intelligence.

And this is the case just because, as stated, the field or Universal Mind is too weak to form intelligences above the ionic and molecular level, but it can unite these small, specialized intelligences into living communities and living civilizations of intelligences, as systems of intelligences, or minds, or cognitive systems.

And if you are a leader in your community or nation, then your primal intelligences might even manage to lead entire regions, nations, and the entire society. And this is how, when you study dictators closely, you find their security, eating, social, and reproductive primal intelligences ruling most of the time, from the top of their cognitive system. And this is exactly how totalitarian regimes are instated, and how exploitation, discrimination, and harassment take place.

We also notice how, if you focus your perception and interaction on the specialization itself, you might end up with a group of robots and machines performing their task throughout the factory. Which is mostly how science considers cells and life in general, as this is the basic, mechanical, algorithmic, consensual first level. But when you focus your perception, understanding, and interconnectivity in meaning instead of specialization, you understand the living, intelligent, harmonious meaning, instead of the dry, mechanical task or specialization.

Since just as you can feel it yourself, your meaning is alive, intelligent, and harmonious, as it comes intrinsically from your intelligences. While the specific task that you perform in the current consensual society might be different, done for financial reasons.

Furthermore, when you consider people for what they do in the family or in society, then you consider them for the tasks that they undergo, even as disposables, as it is the case in many social instances today. But when you consider people as who they are in life and in this world, as the actual living human beings, through their own meanings, talents, needs, achievements, interconnectivity, feelings, success, and fulfillment, you are in the real, living world now, at your third intelligent human level, and not in the Consensual Matrix, at its first consensual dead level.

Let us study next your meaning throughout environments of higher classes of life, as your family, community, society, nation, and civilization. And again, seek to maintain yourself meaningful in life and in this world, in a lively, intrinsic, intelligent manner, but not only specialized, in a first, consensual, mechanical way. Because your loved ones always feel the difference.

3 CHAPTER NAME

Throughout the first part of this book, we have studied your meaning within your organism and cognitive system, as you interact with the outside world. Humans do not live life individually or alone, and this is the case with all living beings. This is not a matter of choice, but Life tends to fill up all environmental niches with her living beings, having them tucked up into each other so tightly, that there is no available spot left where they live. You may study germs within cultures to see how well collective existence is managed throughout life. And this is the case with all living beings, since they use at maximum all resources of the environment. And as we have seen, humans and all living beings fulfill their needs, and this is how they manage to subsist, develop, and alter their environment in order to fulfill their needs faster and more efficiently. Even more niches appear in this manner through the modification of the environment, these niches start being used immediately by newer members, and life goes on.

There are two types of meanings, one within the society, as a specialization meaning, and one in this world, resulted from the interaction with this world, which is the material environment, which is the rest of the surrounding environment found outside the social environment. Similarly, there are two types of interaction with the social and material environment, and this may be symbiotic and parasitic. Therefore, now you have these four types of meanings, and I refer to them as symbiotic or parasitic, in society or in life, and in the entire world.

The problem with living your life within groups, communities, and societies, is the continuous, tedious competition for your specific niche in the environment, and the continuous requirement for a harmonious collective interaction assuring that living beings never work one against another. Study again the same culture of germs, to find it thriving in perfect harmony, just as the cells of your body do, never working one against another. And this is an example of symbiotic meaning in life, maintaining the cooperation and harmony within your society and material environment. While there is an intrinsic intelligent human need to assure symbiotic relationships with the entire human environment.

Your heart has hundreds of millions of cells beating in synchronicity, while they are also cooperating closely with the rest of the cells of the body, since these are specialized, they have a meaning in the organism, and without their meaning or specialized work, the entire heart is never able to do its job, pumping the blood and keeping you alive. If it was not for the cells of your digestive system feeding everyone, or for the cells of your lungs harvesting oxygen, or for the cells of your kidneys filtering blood, then nothing in the organism was possible, and no one could perform their specialization.

Throughout this chapter, we are interested to understand a very similar meaning that humans still manage to fulfill throughout life, which is their specific specialized meaning in society. The human meaning is capable to offer humans a symbiotic relationship within society, yet there are cases of parasitic relationships within human societies, and they are relevant to study. And since there are no real intelligent human societies for us to study but only consensual, utopian, non-viable human societies, we may not state now that intelligent human societies are symbiotic in nature while consensual human societies are parasitic.

We may only state that consensual societies are mechanical or consensual, at the first algorithmic consensual mechanic level. Because through consensus, you cannot reach Life at any of her levels of life, regardless of how much you try. And this is the case just because Life is significantly more complex and therefore more demanding than your specific agreement, or than an entire list of agreements in the Consensual Matrix, since Life is infinite in living characteristics, and you can never match it consensually. Mostly while all agreements end up contorted shortly down the road, just ask the lawyers.

Because politicians may offer you an entire list of promises and agreements, but then only a few months and years down the road, everything becomes contorted, and you have what you had before. And now, with this Consensual Matrix in place for several millennia, just see for yourself what it had become of this world. Since this is the difference between the Golden Ages of Earth, and the Dark Ages.

And now, by studying the three social classes composing society: the Masses, the Brotherhood, and the Elite, we may state that all upper social classes are parasitic, feeding on the lower ones in a hierarchical manner, with the Masses on the bottom, providing everything to them. Similarly, all social layers within the Brotherhood are parasitic and hierarchic in nature, feeding on the lower level ones throughout all hierarchies of the Brotherhood. I refer to this middle social class as the Brotherhood, just because it had originated as a symbiotic society ages and millennia ago. Yet now it is a parasitic hierarchy in itself, an order, and this is how all its members refer to it, as the Order. Which is consensual and hierarchic in nature just as well.

Yet everybody was meaningful, fulfilling, and harmonious long ago, during the Golden Ages of Earth, and not only the Brotherhood. While in the Elite, you have the cruelest of the cruelest ever managing to climb on top of this world, as this is not exactly a living human meaning.

I refer to groups of people as societies, and these include

your work or school social environments, your community environment, nation environment, along with your specific groups of friends and business partners, along with brotherhoods and even larger family environments. These are societies of human beings, all offering you a continuous social environment throughout life, while they form society.

All your social environments are not simply random groups or gatherings of people that you have managed to find so far, but they are living environments as we have seen throughout the book, just as organisms are alive, formed of cells that are also alive. Even more, we have seen how specialized primal intelligences are capable to send you needs that you must fulfill throughout life in order for you to subsist and develop. And now we assume that this is similar with all your outer environments, as these outer environments including society send you continuously natural and social needs that you must fulfill throughout life on behalf of the entire society, only for you and all their members to be able to live together, in harmony and never one against another. This is what meanings are, needs coming from the environment that you must fulfill alongside your own needs, only for all members of that environment to be able to live together.

And this is how you have one baker in society baking the bread, you have one driver to deliver the mail, one policeman to keep order, along with one teacher, one butcher, and one builder. These are specialized humans doing their jobs, and they are working in this manner throughout life on behalf of the rest of this world, day and night, just because they feel this outer need coming from society itself, which is their meaning in society and in this world.

Or this was the case in the intelligent human society. Only living human beings of all classes are intelligent and therefore they are capable to send needs and meanings, therefore we must also assume that society is alive and intelligent and therefore it is capable to send accurate needs and accurate feelings as rewards, and now this is why farmers, drivers, and builders just love their jobs. Right?

Yet it depends, because you feel love when you enter your classroom in the morning and all students are at their desks ready to learn. And this still happens throughout this world, while drivers still love their job mostly on Friday. While it does seem that society is alive and capable to interact with you through meanings and feelings, synchronizing in this manner all its members and therefore rendering them capable to work with each other harmoniously, and never one against another.

Yet people work one against another in this world, since whatever some people produce in southern Asia is transported to North America or South Africa, with over half of those products being discarded during the first week, and with the rest to be discarded in the following months. While people from North America may produce battle equipment that ends up in Asia, destroyed instantly during battles, while killing people of many nations. And this is not at all fulfilling a symbiotic meaning in life, while it might not be exactly the intention that society has from its members.

Similarly, you as an organism want all your cells healthy and happy, you even send them love and care, and it might seem trivial now when you study yourself, but you may notice that there is not a single scratch on your skin, no cell is hurt in your body most of the time, and they work and live within your body and mind just perfectly, cells and intelligences alike.

Why the difference? Why having parasitic and unharmonious meanings in society and in this world? Is it because people are bad and can never live together, and this is why they fight continuously? This is what you learn from all ideologies, while this is never true, because people are similar, mostly good, just because their primal intelligences send them natural needs for harmony and cooperation in the outside world. You still receive extreme social needs for social competition and social supremacy, since the human environment is systematically maintained scarce, while these extreme needs are enough to explain your consensual, hierarchic work environment and school environment. But you receive extreme needs for social competition and social supremacy only at the second developmental level, which is the animal level, not at the third, intelligent human developmental level.

Something is not right in society, but what is it? And this is the case because society is not a natural human environment but a consensual one, of the first developmental level, built on servitude and material benefits. While first level societies are always hierarchic and therefore parasitic. Because you might love your life as a farmer or as a teacher, but when you go to work in the morning for money, to be there for the rest of the day for not too much money, then you do not receive the same love as you once did, when you first started working there years ago. Is society mad at you, and it does not send you love anymore? No, society is consensual, and it might not be alive at all, but only a simple mechanism, since all mechanisms are of the first mechanical algorithmic level. Because money defines your meaning in life now, and not the specific primal social intelligences that we model here. While money and wealth are parasitic in the manner defined by capitalism, which is the current main social ideology of this world, offering to any nation and society all tools and means for the rich to feed on the poor and therefore to get richer continuously throughout life and throughout this world. Capitalism offers discriminatory, parasitic means in life, and it does not matter how other regimes, political parties, societies, and nations call themselves, because as long as they use money and wealth to define all meanings and needs in society, then these are capitalist, and therefore they are parasitic, discriminatory, and exploiting in nature, with the rich exploiting the poor, legally.

But do these assumed primal social intelligences even exist, to be able to send you your natural meanings in a natural, free, genuine society, and therefore for you to be capable to bypass the Consensual Matrix with its hierarchies and money that distribute and manage all social meanings today? Because as we have seen in the previous chapter, the primal intelligences of your cognitive system exist and are alive and conscious just as you are, the conscious intelligence. They send you your inner needs in an intelligent manner and you manage to fulfill them, everything is done for the wellbeing of the entire organism, you work together throughout life keeping the inner harmony, and life goes on happily.

You note how all meanings and all specializations within your family are managed intrinsically, through needs and feelings, exactly as your primal intelligences send these needs and feelings to you. While there is no such thing as an overall family intelligence possessing you at home to instruct you continuously what to do and how to share your tasks and duties. Even more, your specific specializations within your family are done by your own specialized primal intelligences, as your security primal intelligence and eating primal intelligence.

Yet is it possible to have a similar intrinsically motivated behavior in society? Is it possible to be willing and able to work for the entire community or for the entire nation and society through your own intrinsic motivation, not for money or any form of retribution? Yes, certainly, and this is exactly what Ubuntu claims, that you should never follow authorities and currencies throughout life, but only your own needs, feelings, meanings, and determination. Because love and the Divine are always the answer, and you should always follow these closely, since they are your true meanings.

There are countless of ideologies stating the structure of any of these intrinsic free societies. While the Consensual Matrix pays close attention to anyone trying to instate any of these free societies, since if they ever do, then the Consensual Matrix has to dissipate away, and there is no more matrix. So yes, it is possible. Even more, your own intelligent human needs, when you are capable to fulfill them, will always lead you toward the instatement of free human environments and intrinsic motivations, to fulfill your meaning in this world and throughout life.

And you may already receive these meanings but you cannot afford to fulfill them, because it is tedious to tend to yourself and to your entire family, let alone tending for an entire community or society. It sounds nice but very hard to implement, yet it is possible to instate this kind of free societies, if all the people in this world synchronize to discard money and hierarchies at once, and follow their own intrinsic needs and feelings of higher levels and higher classes.

Only that, first you have to have all the people of this world developed at the third, intelligent human level. While nobody is developed at the intelligent human level, while nobody even intends to develop at the third human level. With the Brotherhood and the Elite strongly determined to stay in the Consensual Matrix, and this is the great majority of this world. Because as stated, the Consensual Matrix is flawless and eternal.

Additionally, all souls coming here by the billions are in the Consensual Matrix, under oath and with all ceremonies applied, and they have to remain in the Consensual Matrix by law and duty. And now, if you only attempt to form the genuine human society in any manner, they take you out.

Because when you were little, yes, you had the determination to become president and help this world in every manner, for no retribution at all. Or you wanted to become astronaut and discover new worlds, or to become a doctor to cure this world. Because when you were little, if you grew up in a proper environment, you had the fulfillment of all your lower level needs assured, as your food, security, recovery, socialization, learning, and development, and you were ready and strongly determined to fulfill your intelligent human needs, and through them, to create a perfect intelligent human world, full of righteousness and wellbeing. And this is the living intelligent human society, and you have it in you and ready to implement it in the outside world, if you are only willing to fulfill your intelligent human meaning. And it was only later on, when you discovered lower level needs, that you had to decay to lower developmental levels. And so you may still live your life now in this manner, if this happens to be your case.

And this is why we have to split our model in two now, one for all third level genuine, natural human meanings that might be irrelevant now in a consensual, lower developed world, and one for all first level consensual meanings, assignments, and duties that you have to fulfill in this world.

Let us move one class of life further up, to see if our model still holds for all classes of life. If you live in a large city, as many people do today, preoccupied the entire time with work tasks, money, and consensual social problems, then you might not even know where your community center is, and what it stands for. Because the Consensual Matrix does not want you involved in anything besides your consensual work and ideals, and this is what you always do. It is only during disasters and calamities of all kind that you really manage to integrate yourself within your community. And this is the case not only because you need your community support to get through, because many times, you are the one supporting the entire community during crisis, through your intelligent human meanings, and it adds to your already tedious task of protecting and providing to yourself and to your family.

So why do you do so? Why do you save everybody? Why do you open your fridge and let everyone eat, while it might not be enough food left for yourself later on throughout the crisis? Because there is no electricity, and the food would spoil anyway? Well, no, you simply do so in order to fulfill your intrinsic needs of higher classes. And now, while you read this book, you might find it trivial or utopic, but if you had the chance to be in a real disaster, war, or revolution, now you know how you really work hard and risk your life the entire time in order to protect everybody. And you cannot even imagine doing otherwise, because your higher class meanings and higher level needs are so intense, and when you fulfill them they are so rewarding, that you pursue your true meaning during those dreadful times, without thinking twice.

Because you are at your intelligent human level then, since your entire cognitive system switches you to crisis modes of life. And with no authorities and no matrix around to dictate you anymore, you simply follow your intrinsic meanings in this world, and this is how you behave then.

Why are authorities not around during crisis? Most of them

hide in bunkers, hiding and planning for the future, how to restore order and control, because your community might be isolated now from the Consensual Matrix throughout the disaster, examples are many to give, yet this is always the case. You and your entire area always break free from the Consensual Matrix and from the rest of society during dreadful times, just because the Consensual Matrix never cares to have plans implemented specifically for this kind of circumstances. And this is the case because in any consensual world, you are what you do for that world, you are the specific consensual specialization in that consensual world. And in this manner, you are disposable and easily replaceable, regardless of what you are promised.

As an example, the entire electric grid in North America is vulnerable to larger solar flares and electromagnetic attacks, ready to fail with the slightest nuclear bomb detonated in the atmosphere. And with burned transformers, it cannot restore power for months or years. Yet authorities never care to isolate the grid, even if power failure for such a long time can result in the death of almost everybody. Or this is what the Consensual Matrix claims, because once the electric grid fails, then the Consensual Matrix cannot control the people anymore, communities become independent, humans develop to their intelligent human level, at least many do, and they might even instate an intelligent human society before the Consensual Matrix is reinstated when the crisis is over.

Your own community is your wider neighborhood environment, and it includes the entire habitat, along with all people, all food and resources, and all material and devices necessary throughout life. If the Consensual Matrix was absent today, you were supposed to live your life within your community, most of the time, as an intelligent human being, because you happen to be of the human species, having human abilities and expectations. Without the Consensual Matrix and all its ideologies in place, there are no rules and restrictions about how to fulfill your needs, and therefore nothing and no one can restrict the number of your family. And this is how, without the Consensual Matrix and its ideologies instated, your family is actually the size of your community, since your family is your community in an intelligent human world, where you share everything with everybody in common.

What is wrong with these intelligent human communities, and why should they always be avoided according to authorities, laws, rules, and ideologies? It always relates with illegal sexual interaction happening there with totalitarian rulers. This is exactly what the Consensual Matrix states, the Consensual Matrix destroys these intelligent human communities instantly if they ever appear, and this is exactly why you find none around. If you want to know more about them, just study Ubuntu, since it is not only a computer operating system. Or study the commune of Paris, since centuries ago, Parisians fought in vain in order to reinstate a similar free community the size of a very large city, and the Consensual Matrix killed them. However, those Parisians fought in order to reinstate the commune of Paris, simply because Francs used to live in those parts of this world in big communes spanning large chunks of the continent, with people sharing everything without money for centuries and millennia, throughout entire Golden Ages. And they were probably sharing even their women, since marriages have been instated for about two thousand years, and only in the Western Civilization, while no one knew anything about having to be married, or having to have only one spouse.

But did it really work? Were the French capable to live in free human societies far in the past, before the Consensual Matrix? Just follow the words, because the name 'Franc' should tell you something, since that relates to an intelligent human characteristic. There were other people in this world then, and their names should tell you something else, as the 'Barbarians,' 'Vandals,' 'Russ,' and 'Huns,'.

What is wrong with free societies, if they have worked before? The Consensual Matrix cannot rule you if you ever instate your freedom and self-sufficiency. And without its totalitarian authority over you, the Consensual Matrix dissipates in thin air instantly, since the Consensual Matrix is consensual and lives in your words and statements, in your ideologies and in your tacit or explicit agreement to be part of it. In fact, it is enough now to state in any manner that you are the living human being and not the consensual corporation, and you are not part of the Consensual Matrix anymore. Just put away all documents and identity cards that have your name in uppercase letters, and it is impossible for the Consensual Matrix to have you. And what happens next? You cannot work anymore, since they never allow you there as a living human being. You cannot use money, you cannot get your pension, you cannot get your money from your bank account, you have to provide for yourself without money, which you mostly do anyway, so yes, it is always possible. Even more, if there are more as you stating their freedom and human rights throughout this world, then you may form an intelligent human environment. And this is alive, just as your family at home.

Even more, the Consensual Matrix has plans to exterminate you entirely once you show signs of higher development. There is a current movement in this world toward adopting an intelligent human environment and lifestyle, as everything develops on the current informational platform made possible by the Internet and by smartphones. These alone are capable to connect people directly, allowing them to share information while relying on their own ability and authority, bypassing the Consensual Matrix. The Consensual Matrix is currently capable to control this technological connectivity among people, yet not for long. And this is why you hear more about a new world war, about times of revelation, about the culling, about mass extermination, about the end of this world, and about birds of fire being reborn from their own ashes. And with all these wars and pandemics around, you never know.

How exactly do you find your own specialization in this world? Do you choose it yourself, or it is your true meaning, your destiny? And if you do not choose exactly that one, you might live your entire life in vain. What intelligences decide your meaning in life? We have two types of societies to consider. A natural one similar to the intelligent human community presented above, and a consensual one, similar to what you are very familiar with, since you are in the Consensual Matrix wherever you are.

As stated, it is always better to live life in agreement with those around, than in chaos and destruction. However, there are many problems with the Consensual Matrix. Because it is contorted very easily, and in this contorted manner, it can never offer you consensus, agreements, and cooperation, but only loss and disagreement. Which is always the case with the Consensual Matrix, just study the politicians and the rest of the public workers. Another problem is that, through the Consensual Matrix, dreadful higher beings manage to control Earth, as it is the case with the higher being controlling the invisible kingdom, and through the invisible kingdom, the Brotherhood and the Elite. While this is the great majority of this world. Which means that most of this world does not believe in our Creator, in Life, or in the Deity, but in some higher being. This is why the invisible kingdom does not even recognize the Creator of this world, acting against it. With the Creator of this world deleting them in mass, along with this entire world, and along with all the worlds above that he had created. And there will be no more.

Within consensual societies, you simply find a job, and that is your meaning in this world, to make money and to provide for yourself and for your family. This is what you do, while at work, you perform your required duties, and you care less if the shirts that you manufacture today are meant to help others in society, or if the electricity that your plant generates is meant to help others throughout life, as long as you receive your salary. Or you still do, since you brag at times, about how important your job is, and it even makes you proud. It is love that you feel then, and this is your reassurance that your job is your meaning in life, besides your family and gaining money. And this is now your life, your reason in life. And even so, even with the Consensual Matrix instated, life in this world remains highly desirable up there throughout higher worlds, for its difficulty mostly. And as a soul, you have to be capable to be able to go through an entire lifetime here on Earth, since it is hard.

If you seek money, power, influence, and continuous material pleasure, since these define now your meaning in life within consensual social environments, if you happen to live your life on lower developmental levels to match them, then what exactly sets your meanings in life within free, intelligent human societies that have no authorities and no currencies to regulate them? Currently, as all ideologies describing these free intelligent human societies, there are very strong rules to abide by, as these rules are the ones controlling your life, they are your authority. And even more, the specific authorities set in place to instate these rules are your new authorities, within these 'free,' 'intelligent human societies. 'Free' means no authorities and no rules, since rules and authorities lead to servitude. And this is why you have to be at an intelligent human level in order to be able to live and subsist in a free, intelligent human society, or in any free, intelligent human environment.

It is nice when you find your meaning in life and in this world and when you are allowed to fulfill it freely, since life is very nice. While the people fulfilling their needs through you are very happy just as well, and this is called human fulfillment, human meaning, and human harmony. But if you ever force yourself to follow a meaning that is not yours, then your life does not make sense at all, it lacks meaning, and you should never do so. However, if it is ever anything that you are highly capable to do for this world and this world needs it badly, while you still do not have the heart for it, you will see how your own primal specialized intelligences will motivate you to do so anyway. And you will do so for the rest of your life and you will always love it, because you will feel love the entire time, intrinsic love, and this is your meaning in life.

Because if you are a laborer tending to screws all day long while you dream of being a poet and bring your art to this world, then screws and factories might not be your specialization or meaning in this world. And if it is not, while all the people around tell you otherwise, then you are not capable to fulfill your human needs that way. And if you are not capable to fulfill your human needs, then that is not at all an intelligent human society, but an impostor, a surrogate. And with everybody experiencing the same, it will decay rapidly to an animal society, slavery society, or addiction society. Or this is always the case with all 'free' societies that people still try to implement throughout this world, and it never seems to work. Or because tight laws and authorities 'motivating' everybody to work for free all life long never works. Because your needs want you to develop and do what you really want, while the tight laws of your new society state otherwise, and it makes everything worse than it was before.

Yet in the real world, the Consensual Matrix makes sure that you remain at work all day long, and this is why I considered that you also have now to work eight or ten hours a day in the factory, every day, while this should not be the case. Because in the real world, the Consensual Matrix controls your working hours simply by discarding whatever you produce at work in order to produce it repeatedly, to keep you preoccupied at work. And this is why all products break down within weeks or months and you have to manufacture newer ones, and this is why food is wasted almost entirely in every manner throughout the developed world, only for you to work in the fields some more. Because within free societies, your intelligent human needs will never allow you to work in vain, but will make you research better technologies, power sources, and automated procedures, only for people not to have to perform unnecessary work. Because this is exactly why your intelligences do not allow you to work at the factory screwing bolts all day long, because the factory itself is harmful for the human environment, while your intelligences push you through your intelligent human needs to find new, better technologies the entire time.

We may study this example closely now, to see how, when

you reach adulthood, you do not really have to engage in an unwanted position at the nearby factory. Because in an intelligent human society, that factory would not even be there. Yet you would be already engaged in technological research since childhood, or in sports development, in writing complex computer applications, or in performing art this entire time. Because within intelligent human societies, you never stop studying and developing once you reach adulthood, but you continue in this manner throughout life, just because higher learning and higher development are intelligent human needs, and you have to fulfill them continuously throughout life. And the reward is significant when those around become interested in what you do, when they find it relevant and useful, when they read your books and they learn something new from them, when they use your new technology and it works, or when they read your poems and sing your songs. Because what you do in life and in this world is relevant. While the amount of love that you feel then is significant, and everything makes sense, everything has meaning, you have a reason in this world, and everything is wonderful.

Because within intelligent human societies, life is never about rendering you constrained or motivated to work in a specific field, specialization, or meaning, but it is the other way around, because many times, you struggle to implement your work and research in the intelligent human society, since this gives you meaning in life. You are not interested in this work anymore if it is not accepted, since it is irrelevant if it is not useful in society, but you become more interested in this specific acceptance in this world of your own contribution to this world, of your own study, of your own idea, and this is what you focus your attention now, hoping to make it work. Even your primal specialized intelligences stop rewarding you with love for your work and creations if none of it is accepted in this world, which is, if you are not capable to contribute to society. And it might seem irrelevant to you now, but if you keep failing to find your meaning or specialization in society and therefore if you cannot fulfill your intelligent human needs, then you start to be punished more, until you die.

Yet it does not have to be poetry, art, or philosophy, to give meaning to this world. You may tend to children as they grow up, or you may cook if you happen to show more interest in food. You may design cars or clean up the streets while you try new work, you may help anyone around who needs help, you may do everything, and if you ever feel love for what you do, anything related to helping this world, then your life will be spared. This is not a belief, that you will die if you do not find and tend to your meaning in society and in this world or to any work in society and in this world, but it is the case and it happens with all species, including humans. Because without love, without people, without inner and outer recognition in this world, without motivation and meaning in life and in this world, you truly feel worse every day, and you die. Because without reward feelings, you will produce so many free radicals in you, recycling your entire body so rapidly, that you will die of any sickness related to old age then, by the end of the year.

This should not be the case, because you will always help around the community anyway. Even more, it will not happen while you are still young, because while you are young, your primal reproductive intelligence will give you a very clear meaning in life, to reproduce and to tend to all the children, to care for them, and teach them well until adulthood. It is only decades later, when you are not accepted anymore as a favorable reproduction partner, and when children are grown up and now others have to tend to the young ones, that you have nothing else to do, and your stay here in this world might be over.

It is the same with all species, since in general, animals die after their next generation reaches adulthood. There are some cases when animals get to live longer, as wheals, dolphins, apes, and probably elephants do, because they have to tend to the second generation, to the offspring of their offspring. Yet human beings have higher needs to tend to, and as long as they are useful to society, as long as they feel love, then they may remain alive. And then, whenever they stop working, they slowly start to fade away.

What we want to study now is how exactly you contribute to society once you find your meaning in society and in this world. Is there a specific working pattern that you have to follow throughout life?

As you may notice, you already find these cases in our current society, as consensual as it may be. Today, you already find hundreds of thousands of artists and writers who publish their work online after years of hard work, to have only one viewer a week or a month and nothing more, while they are entirely convinced that it is real art or real literature, since it exceeds in artistic quality and ideas whatever bestsellers offer today. Yet still, no one is ever interested in their work. And so this world reads garbage in books and admires trash in art, while all original writers and artists create their work in vain or they stop working altogether, disappointed of an entire world.

And now, if you as an intelligence are incapable to specialize because your cognitive system does not recognize you because it does not need your service, you simply cease in this manner to exist. It is not a rule, to die instantly once you have finished your job in this world, but without your contribution to this world, you do not mean anything to this world, you are not part of this world, you are not part of the Divine, and Existence cannot define you anymore, even though you are not dead yet. It is the same with intelligences within cognitive systems, with cells within organisms, with animals within all animal groups, and even with some people today in this world, since they cease to exist when they do not contribute to this world. Death itself is not the absence of life as science and education make you believe, but death itself is an invention of life, meant to discard all the unwanted ones. And this is why living beings grow old, not because their minds and bodies are too old since the human body is capable to regenerate itself indefinitely, but they grow old because there are specific mechanisms embedded in all living beings made to kill them under specific circumstances, mostly when they do not have a meaning in this world anymore. Since the most important circumstance is when you are not useful for your kind and for this world anymore. And this is exactly why older people try their best to find their place around children today, while society shoos them away, because that is their last job that they have left. And if they do not act as they are needed in this world, then they have to die away.

This is why intelligences are eager to specialize, because they do not exist otherwise, and they have to go back to the field. And now if the intelligences of your cognitive system have no more meaning in this world through you, if you truly fail society and cannot integrate, cannot be useful, and cannot find your meaning, then they die whenever you die, and life is over, for you and for them. While they motivate you in every manner to find your place in this world, rewarding you when you are successful, and this is exactly what you do. And this intrinsic motivation is sufficient to determine you to contribute to this world, by far more than you do today through money and hierarchies that tell you exactly what to do. While you feel lazy and awkward the entire time. Because once drugs and cheap entertainment are over and dissipate away with the Consensual Matrix when it is gone, then your intelligences will motivate you intrinsically, naturally, to participate in everything in this world, and you will love it.

Yet you only have to take away drugs from the world, and the Consensual Matrix dissipates away, since without drugs, everybody seeks to fulfill their needs and meanings, only to have something to do. And once you form and maintain the intelligent human environment through your needs and meanings, you do not need money and social power anymore, because your meanings are very fulfilling. Yet the Consensual Matrix keeps drugs instated in the world even by force, so you will always take drugs, you will always neglect or contort your meanings, you will always be in the Consensual Matrix, and therefore you will always be exploited and you will always exploit others.

What do drugs have to do with all these? Should drugs not be free in free societies? At least wine? No, not at all. All intrinsic motivation meant to determine you to do everything that you currently do is based on good feelings, while all good feelings are limited within your cognitive system, and you either receive them as rewards throughout the fulfillment of your needs and meanings, or you receive them from drugs and entertainment. In other words, you cannot be in the zero addicted mode of life and in any other mode of life simultaneously, just because you do not have enough good feelings for all, since your feelings are limited within your cognitive system. In fact, you cannot even receive more good feelings through drugs than you usually receive, just because good feelings are limited within your cognitive system. And now, once drugs give you your good feelings freely, you learn to ignore your cognitive system, you are not motivated to fulfill your needs and meanings in this world and in society, and therefore you do not even exist for this world and for society anymore. This is why it is called the zero level of development, because you count nothing for Life and for this world.

Of all problems in this world, drugs are the worst, for this reason, because they steal your life away, and so you do not count anymore in this world. This is why people leave you when you are addicted, because you are not there for them anymore, you do not have feelings for them anymore, you do not count for them anymore, and it does not really make a difference if they leave you or not. While drugs also destroy your cognitive system, they kill your intelligences and therefore they remove their abilities if they ever survive. And this is what drugs do to you, throughout consensual worlds and throughout free societies.

The reason why the Consensual Matrix uses drugs today is because you lack possibilities to fulfill many of your natural needs in the Consensual Matrix, and drugs help you compensate your missing feelings from your life. While drugs also help destroy the higher side of your cognitive system, for various reasons. However, without drugs, and with full awareness of your human needs, you will always find ways to fulfill your human needs even in the current society, as you do now.

Let us now try to model all intelligences of all classes of life, in order to see if there are individual overall intelligences within society, sending you social meanings that define your specialization for life and keep you motivated throughout life while you do your work for the rest of this world.

For example, the specific intelligences forming you the conscious intelligence specialize in logic, creativity, choice, decision-making, and mental modeling. All cognitive systems are relatively similar, all having intelligences of relatively similar specializations, and they resemble to your own cognitive system, with the eating intelligence, developmental intelligence, security intelligence, and reproductive intelligence. Now, when you gather a multitude of cognitive systems as it is the case when you go from one class of life to a higher one, as from one cell to an entire culture of cells, you have a multitude of similarly specialized intelligences, yet they are unique, and therefore they do not fulfill tasks, needs, and meanings in similar manners as computers do. And they do not work together in mass as robots do, but they subdue and help each other or they rule and constrain each other, depending on their developmental level. While their behavior and development depends on the conditions of their environment. Therefore, according to each environmental condition, all intelligences of all cognitive systems will perform tasks and fulfill meanings in a specific manner and under specific cognitive structures, but with the most competent and pertinent intelligence always leading or ruling the entire cognitive system in a genuine cognitive pyramid of power and competence, as it happens in society with the social pyramid of power.

And just because cognitive systems are composed of primal intelligences that are in themselves systems of intelligences formed of intelligences that are in themselves systems of intelligences down to the last cognitive procedures, and because the environment changes continuously, forcing this highly diverse cognitive system to shift itself from one mode to another and from one developmental level to another in order to match the environment, now you can never consider that the specific cognitive system belongs to the specific physical body or class of life where it is found, just because the specific intelligence ruling them at one moment or another according to the environmental conditions comes from very low cognitive levels and systems, and it does not belong to the high class of life that you are studying. And since this is always the case, because all environments behave similarly, since they are alive themselves, and they undergo a similar cognitive behavior, being comprised of similar individual intelligences caught within similar changing cognitive systems, you can never consider that classes of life have intelligences on their own, but only that they are using the most pertinent intelligences coming from below, from lower class levels.

The cells of your organism are an example here. The first class of organic life is the cell, yet since the organic life has plasmatic and ionic forms of life at its base, there are still other class levels below cells. Cells are of two types: prokaryotes and eukaryotes. Prokaryotes are the usual bacteria, they live independently, and they are twenty times smaller than eukaryotes, which are the cells composing your organism. When you study eukaryotes, you find mitochondria in there, and these are in fact prokaryotes living within eukaryotes continuously, specialized now in charging ATP molecules to be used throughout the cell. ATPs are the source of charge and therefore energy within the cell. Biology considers only prokaryotic cells alive, but not the eukaryotes composing your organism, even though they are by far more complex than prokaryotes. However, prokaryotes are alive, and they have their own intelligences, just as all cells do. While the cells of your body that already contain eukaryotes are not considered alive on their own, but only the entire organism is considered alive by science today. Yet science entirely is an ideology, based on the unanimous consensus of its main scientist.

If you have a physical body capable to form, hold, and maintain inner realities and intelligences within, then you have life. All cells are alive, along with all cellular components. Your organism is composed of five or seven trillion cells, more or less, depending on your weight. They are alive, they live together, and they are intelligent, while their own cellular intelligences form now your primal intelligences, including you. All primal intelligences are systems of intelligences on their own, of cellular intelligences, which are also systems of intelligences, found in all cellular components as they interact with the field within cells. Furthermore, these inner intelligences are systems of intelligences themselves, down to simple ions. Because cellular components as RNAs and proteins are formed of amino acids, which are formed of ions, while these are capable to hold intelligences, down to the field itself. These intelligences, when they unite to form systems of intelligences, never combine and never lose their uniqueness, but they only specialize within their system of intelligences. When systems of intelligences combine, these also specialize in similar specializations as the smaller intelligences did while forming themselves. But now, by having a multitude of smaller specialized intelligences of the same specialization, the most pertinent intelligence climbs on top of the cognitive system to do the job whenever its own specialization happens to be significant in the outside environment. And this is how, if they are pertinent enough, intelligences from within lower classes of life reach out and become now pertinent and capable enough to rule or lead higher and higher classes, one above another, as far as possible.

And this is exactly the case with you, the conscious intelligence, and with all your specialized primal intelligences, since you come from your lowest classes of life. You were pertinent enough to come from lower class levels in order to lead now your entire neuron, then your entire area on your prefrontal cortex, then from there you are pertinent enough to be the conscious intelligence of the entire organism leading trillions of cells throughout life, while from there you are pertinent enough to lead an entire family, an entire community, an entire factory or an entire political party, an entire city, or an entire nation.

And this is how your organism as a whole does not exactly have its own overall intelligences, but all its intelligences come from below, from the ionic form of life, molecular form of life, and from the cellular form of life. They are simple cellular intelligences working together, exactly as people work together within society, while forming society. And when you study cells in a similar manner, you find them lacking intelligences on their own, since all overall cellular intelligences spanning the entire cell are in fact only systems of smaller intelligences, composed of the very small intelligences of all cellular components, the ions and molecules of the ionic form of life and the molecular form of life.

And this is the case class of life below class of life, down to the slightest components of all these cellular components and below, to subatomic and subnuclear forms of life, if there are any. And then further on down to the field itself or the Universal Mind, if there are any elemental intelligences living directly in the field itself. And you can go lower than this, because the field itself is at the base of the spacetime continuum of this world, it is embedded in it, while the continuum of this world is formed, held, and maintained in the matrix that holds our entire world in its intelligent encoding, matrix that is held directly by our higher reality, just as your brain holds your mind here in this world, or as computer hardware holds computer software here in our world in a digital matrix created and maintained by the multitude of switches within the motherboard.

And this is how all intelligences of all cognitive systems of this world originate through the field in our upper reality. This is where they come from, there is where all souls and higher beings live, and they may pass in a similar manner from one reality to another as they wish, coming all the way up from the Divine itself, if this is the case. And since these intelligences define your meaning in life and in this world today through feelings of love, then love and the Divine are always the answer.

There is a difference between realities and classes of life, since we consider life divided into classes of life here within our world, as cells, organisms, species, and societies. While we consider the wider world formed of a multitude of realities, one within another, as our higher reality forms, holds, and maintains our world. While within our world, brains hold minds within lower realities, while in a similar manner, systems of intelligences hold the intelligences forming them within even lower realities, which may hold even smaller intelligences within even lower realities.

And this is how upper classes of life are not exactly alive, but their components and members give them life and intelligence, while forming and therefore occupying them.

One consequence of your cells being alive is the fact that the egg formed at the moment of conception is alive itself, it is a human being, it has human rights, and therefore nobody may interfere with its life. And now the Consensual Matrix avoids considering this, only to be able to keep abortions legal.

And now, upper social classes of life and therefore upper environments are not alive in themselves, but their members and components are alive, giving them life. Just as the human cells give life to the entire human organism, while living human beings give life to their family continuously, or to the entire human society, or to the entire world. Similarly, all living beings on Earth give life to Mother Earth. And therefore, all meanings come from human beings themselves, from their cognitive system, and from the primal intelligences depending on the required specialization. And therefore, these specialized primal intelligences are capable not only to coordinate all organisms throughout life through the multitude of needs and feelings, but they are capable to make organisms alter their world and social environment as they interact with it while fulfilling their needs, in order to render it more suitable to fulfill their needs. And this is what meanings in life and in this world are, a systematic work on the outer environment to render it capable to fulfill all needs easier, faster, and more efficiently. While from the perspective of this entire environment, meanings are seen as a specialized work benefiting all members of the environment.

There is more to study here, since all your primal intelligences do not die, but are transferred at the moment of conception wholly from generation to generation, from civilization to civilization, from species to species, from form of life to form of life, and even from one reality to another. This means that all your intelligences have been here in this world throughout the ages of Earth when the Consensual Matrix was absent, and when humanity was very developed. History might suffer of amnesia today, yet your primal intelligences remember it well, and now they send you these developmental needs, to achieve what was the case ages ago. And these are the needs and meanings now that you receive, based on those successful times, when your own genetic line was very successful, within that specific intelligent human environment, and this is what your own primal intelligences want you to achieve.

And this is our answer, since there are not outside social intelligences sending you your meanings, but your own primal intelligences do, according to their own inner specialization within the organism. Since they are capable in this manner, through your specialized meanings, to ted to similar, homologue social specializations in the outside world, in an intelligent human society, and this is the kind of needs that you now receive. And despite of their intrinsic nature, your needs and meanings are pertinent enough to bring back those successful times, when the intelligent human family span this world, with no Consensual Matrix present, but only family members, the intelligent human society.

And therefore, all meanings in life and in this world are intrinsic in nature, and you have them within, just as spirituality states the entire time. This means that you should be always allowed to create your environment according to your inner needs and feelings, and you should never be constrained by laws, authorities, and ideologies to behave in any other way, or they interfere in this manner with your human rights to fulfill your needs, and they infringe the higher laws. And as we have seen, the Consensual Matrix does not accept you as a living human being, but only as a consensual corporation that is not alive, and therefore that has no rights. And it is you signing all forms stating that you represent that corporation even throughout life, and when you do so, you enter the Consensual Matrix.

And now study the Consensual Matrix entirely, as it is formed and exists, and as it uses you and the entire world, to see it mimicking the entire existential model of realities, classes of life, individual members, selves, and consensual rights called privileges within the Consensual Matrix. The Consensual Matrix is a genuine consensual reality and someone had to know this entire model of the wider world, of life, of all interconnectivities, of all developmental levels, of all statuses, rights, intelligences, and of all developmental levels throughout the wider world, because the Consensual Matrix stands relevant, legal, and pertinent through all these, managing in this manner to twist the higher laws and turn them entirely on its behalf, and managing in this manner to exploit and exterminate you even as a highly developed living being. While you know nothing about these, and while you never even suspect them.

Meanings are simply needs of higher classes, which you fulfill on behalf of your family, society, and nation. As stated previously, you live your life within a multitude of modes of life and on various developmental levels, according to your immediate environment. During crisis, as droughts, wars, and famines, when it is hard to find food, once you feel hungry and cannot fulfill your need, your primal eating intelligence climbs at the top of your cognitive system, claiming authority and controlling the entire cognitive system from there, since food is then imperative, and only your eating intelligence is capable to find it, through you, the conscious intelligence. You are switched immediately to your famine or overstocking mode of life in this manner, and you have to live your life from then on preoccupied with food. You have to find food, eat everything, and whatever you eat, it is stored within you as fat. You still feel hungry despite of how much you eat, and you deposit everything as fat and you gain weight, until food is again abundant in the outside world, and you are switched back to your other modes of life, depending on circumstances and on the needs that you have to fulfill. It is more likely that you are switched to your recovery mode of life, to tend to your wounds and illnesses. While until not too long ago, this was a normal kind of life pattern.

And it is important to know your current mode of life, why you are in it, what you have to do in order to cooperate, or how to shift away from it to a more favorable mode of life, if needed. If you are on a diet, you will be shifted to your famine mode of life or to your fat overstocking mode of life, since it seems that for some time, there is not enough food in this world, because you stopped eating. Therefore, there must be another famine, war, or calamity coming, as you notice in all movies, since they are the same. And so you end up gaining more weight just by confusing your cognitive system, while this is a common theme today. Yet if you are young, vibrant, and healthy, it is more likely that you are kept in the adult mode of life continuously, so you may reproduce abundantly throughout life, now that you manage to fulfill all your needs, and that you manage to remain strong, good looking, and healthy. Or this is what your primal intelligence always intends. And this is the kind of life that you now live.

What can you do? You might be happy with your adult mode of life, and live your life in this manner in your adult mode of life continuously, at the second developmental level. Yet if it happens that you want to live your life at the third intelligent human level instead, in order to fulfill your human needs, then you have to manage to ignore the multitude of your modes of life, and to avoid them in any manner. Make sure that you eat enough during your main meals, to last you until the next meal. Do the same with all your lower level needs, have them fulfilled by default. And try to ignore as much as you can your adult mode of life, if it happens that you do not intend to have children right then. Because if you intend to have children, then you may shift yourself to the adult mode of life if you are not already there, since this is easy to do.

And so you shift easily to higher modes of life, as learning or performing art, or helping around. You may also notice that when you are in higher level modes of life, and on higher developmental levels, your reproductive primal intelligence leaves you alone, since higher needs and higher meanings are usually privileged. Even more, higher needs of higher classes that we call meanings are even more privileged, and more rewarded.

Why are these called today meanings, reasons, purposes, and destinies but not needs of higher classes of life? Because no one ever models them in an intelligent manner in order to find out what they truly are, but only empirically. And it only seems that these meanings come from higher social environments, while they are intrinsic, coming from your most pertinent specialized intelligences that now are capable to control the outside environment through you. And this is exactly how you find your meaning, you simply fulfill these needs of higher and higher classes as they apply to you, and whichever need of higher class you happen to receive the most, if the people around find it pertinent, and if you prefer it just as well, then that is your meaning.

For example, you have a normal childhood and you do not think exactly of what you are going to do when you grow up. Your parents never push you to specialize, since they are busy at work. Consequently, your parents are not too capable to repair complicated things, as computers and other appliances, and because you have the time, you repair them yourself, since you never receive new ones anyway. You develop your skills, your neighbors and friends ask you to help them with their computers, you always improve, and without knowing it, now you are an expert in computers. You may charge money for your specialized service, and if you do so, you enter the Consensual Matrix, and everything that you feel from then on is love for money. Your second choice is to refuse retribution, and you feel love from now on, every time you help anyone with their computers.

This might seem irrelevant, but once you join the Consensual Matrix, you have enough money to afford drugs along with the fulfillment of all adult needs, and so you encounter the most common dreadful problems. Yet if you do not charge for your computer service, you have enough love and happiness and you do not really need drugs and therefore servitude. And now, whenever you have a problem yourself with any other specialization, you can always find help, the most pertinent help, with no retribution, and this is how you manage to fulfill your needs. Or this would be the case if you knew everything about the Consensual Matrix, about the human needs and meanings, about societies and specializations, and about drugs, feelings, and rewards, because the Consensual Matrix keeps all these hidden from you.

And again, you notice how capable the Consensual Matrix is, because it knows exactly what knowledge to keep hidden from you, how to keep you in lower developmental levels, how to keep your environment altered in order to stop you from developing, and how to stop you from improve your environment to favor you. The Consensual Matrix knows everything necessary to keep you at the exact developmental level that you are, and exactly within the proper hierarchies of society that you can never escape, as though it knows everything pertinent that you should already know, and uses it now in order to stop you from learning it. The Consensual Matrix never informs you of any of these through science and education as it should, but it knows how to alter science and education in order to use them as forms of indoctrination, in order to keep you down some more. And now, when you look above throughout the social pyramid of power, you may see who or what kind of people stand at the top. And if these are the ones controlling the Consensual Matrix, then they must be very capable. While destroying an entire world.

We want to know now what happens next, once you have your specialization or meaning in your social environment. Will you keep it for life? Yes, why not? You actually undergo an entire developmental pattern throughout life. First, you find your meaning, as teaching specific knowledge, or repairing computers, or cooking, or giving birth to children and raising them, since there is one meaning in this world for all your needs and specialized intelligences. Your specialized intelligences act through you and reach your society directly, they do all the work for you many times, and this is called talent. Yet this is the case at all class levels, since the most pertinent specialized intelligences always emerge from the lower classes of life, to reach past you and act with the same pertinence on society. Just as you the conscious intelligence manage to coordinate an entire organism now, as it interacts with the outside world. And if you happen to be a leader, then you manage to act on higher and higher social classes yourself, the conscious intelligence. But if you specialize in cooking, as becoming a chef, then it is your most pertinent eating intelligence working throughout life, and it is the same with all meanings in society.

What is your best meaning and what should you choose? And more importantly, who exactly decides which one is your most pertinent specialized intelligence? These two questions have the same answer, and you may already know it. First, those around chose you for your talent to repair computers, for your talent to cook, or for your talent to write, paint, or make videos. Secondly, there was a gap in this world, a social niche, a need for your services and specialization, and this is why your specialization, work, or contribution to your society was accepted. It was probably a coincidence, or you have developed your talent on purpose, in order to fill up that social gap, that social need, which is more of a social niche.

And this is the case in all environments, since every time there are open niches, intelligences show up from around or from the classes of life bellow to fill them up with their new specialized expertise in that exact new field. Entire organisms, species, and classes of species develop in this manner, through these newly specialized intelligences happy to fill up the needed new specializations, if they actually know what to do. And through them, no one goes extinct.

Which is also your case, because if you do not know what to do, then you cannot actually fulfill that particular specialized meaning. But now with the current consensual Brotherhood assigning all social branches and social specializations for financial benefits, exploitation, and social influence, this destroys the world, since it overrules exactly these capable specialized intelligences, and therefore it overrules exactly your meaning in society, in life, and in the world. And now you dislike the consensual assignment that the Brotherhood gives you, while your own talent and meaning remain neglected and unused, keeping you unfulfilled. Since this is why the current society feeds you drugs in large amounts, to compensate.

This simple model is capable enough to explain the development of life throughout species, more than the theory of evolution, because each change in the environment is not exactly a trial of what species must die and what species survives, but of what intelligence to fill up that specific opportunity to specialize in a brand-new task or ability of the entire organism or cognitive system.

And whenever this happens, species do not change into something entirely new, but species always use old parts of themselves, morph them, and use them for the new tasks, along with all its inner intelligences that now are responsible with the new task, meaning, need, and activity, in order to be able to cope with the environment.

As stated above, your most difficult task is finding your social niche. This is your specialization in this world, your meaning in life, or your reason to be alive. You are still fulfilling your other needs, but since you perform your new task for others or for the entire society, now your specific specialized intelligence has the chance to work through you toward fulfilling needs coming from the entire family, community, city, or nation. And it is not at all doing extra tedious work or volunteering, but it is an opportunity for more of these specialized intelligences of your cognitive system to help with your new task. They reward you abundantly for what you do, while for them, you gave them the opportunity to exist in this world, to be unique, and even more, to tend to unique tasks in the outside world, as this is highly treasured within cognitive systems.

And examples are many to give, because writers will wake up at two or three in the morning to write all day long, eating only twice a day and never leaving the house for weeks in a row while writing. Or doctors will stay awake day and night, surgery after surgery, only to fulfill their meaning, while never complaining, never asking for retribution and rewards, just fulfilling their meaning. And this is the case at all class levels, because your cells will cooperate with your most tiring tasks, postponing their division, maintenance, and recovery, just for you, just for you to finish your match of tennis, or just for you to finish playing outside, never asking for water or food, never asking to rest. And with your parents calling you to eat the entire time, yet you were never hungry.

It is also possible that you are helped to find your meaning in society. Education should teach you everything about your specialization, developing you accordingly in order for you to be able to fulfill your meaning in life. This is the first step of your developmental pattern. During the second step, you develop continuously at work, finding newer and newer procedures within your profession. Your third step is to find someone else to teach your specialization to, at your turn. And during the fourth step of your developmental pattern, you simply exit the scene and allow the young ones to take your place. This developmental pattern is embedded intrinsically within your cognitive system, and now your primal specialized intelligence sends you these specific types of needs regarding your meaning.

And this is why you are eager to learn as a child in every manner, even through playing, while your entire organism, including your brain, specializes in your domain just as well, in order to be able to keep up with your specialization throughout life. Psychology calls this 'plasticity,' since neurons develop their neural connections according to the specific cognitive tasks and abilities that you learn as a child. And if you learn foreign languages as a child, then this might be your specialization now, for life, since no one will be better than you at foreign languages, just because if you do not learn these as a child, you may never be able to learn them so perfectly. Or if you do not learn to speak, to walk, or to reason as a child for various reasons, you might not be able to perform these as an adult, all having to do with the plasticity of the brain. Or if you do not learn to use your higher cognitive abilities, you might never be able to use them throughout life. Or if you engage in adult activities when you grow up, then this might be what interests you for life, and you might succeed in this manner to have and raise many children.

And then when you grow old, it is the other way around, because most of your higher needs relate to teaching others everything that you know, mostly your own specialization. And this is significant to consider, since you are now among the most competent at what you do. Yet as all your needs, this need for teaching and training others when you grow older is embedded in your cognitive system and you are ready to fulfill it even continuously, if you can only find anyone to sit down and listen to you. While these needs are very hard to fulfill, because everybody has to work and make money today, not necessarily to listen to you. While you are ready to teach everything that you know and can do, since you have been successful at it your entire life. And since it seems that children need to know all these, or this is what your primal intelligences assure, now they send you to find children, to be around children, to talk to children, to teach them everything that you know, and this is hard to fulfill today. Because the Consensual Matrix takes all the children away in order to indoctrinate them in every manner, through schools and TV programs, and you can never be around children anymore in order to teach them everything that your own specialized intelligences want them to learn. Because children are forming their plasticity right then, and the Consensual Matrix wants to catch them at the right time to indoctrinate them, because the Consensual Matrix lives in them and in everybody else, at all ages. And even more, if the Consensual Matrix ever catches you around children, it blames you of everything and it confines you men with men and women with women throughout jails and prisons, so you cannot reproduce and have children yourselves. Therefore, you have to skip this meaning, rendering the Masses extinct, and you have not much left to do in life but to take drugs as everybody else.

But is this world divided into good people and bad people? No, not at all, since they receive similar needs, and have similar tasks to perform throughout life. It is only the Consensual Matrix sending consensual needs to people while indoctrinating them in the process, making for a significant difference in the human behavior throughout this world and throughout time. And now nothing that you see in your outside environment makes sense according to natural laws, while everything goes against your own natural needs, creating all environmental conditions going in one direction, toward your own exploitation and extermination. While blaming you for everything the entire time. And it takes an extraordinary ability for someone or something to contort the Consensual Matrix and do this to an entire world.

Let us now move along to the next chapter, in order to use our model to study higher meanings in life, related to higher beings and higher environments.

4 HIGHER MEANINGS AND HIGHER EXPECTATIONS

We may climb the existential ladder now, to reach higher worlds and higher environments. But let us look back shortly to see what we have found so far, in order to give us a solid base for this last part of our model, the study of our higher meanings in life and in the wider world.

As seen, we have one self, one meaning, and one identity for each one of our worlds and environments that we inhabit, many times simultaneously. To start now with this world, and to define it shortly, everything within our real world exists here in an objective, material manner, and this includes all objects, organisms, living beings, air, water, dust, rocks, mountains, along with the entire electromagnetic and gravitational field, electromagnetic radiation including light, along with electricity. The rest is abstract and not objectively real, and it might be subjectively real, in which case it exists in lower realities held by our world, or highjectively real, if it is part of any higher reality holding our world, just as reality holds its multitude of inner realities, as mind inner realities and computer inner realities. And since existence is relative in its three natures: subjective, objective, and highjective, as everything seems subjective in nature within our inner realities, the same way everything here from this world seems subjective in nature from the perspective of our higher beings found in our higher realities. And just as all higher beings and higher realities seem highjective in nature as seen from our world, similarly, all inner beings and intelligences from all our inner worlds perceive and understand us here in our world in a highjective manner.

Meanings may also be subjective, objective, and highjective, while all your cognitive meanings are subjective in nature. These are your inner meanings that you as a conscious intelligence have within your cognitive system, as cooperating through the accurate fulfillment of your needs with all your primal intelligences, or maintaining the inner harmony within your cognitive system. You fulfill these cognitive meanings through your inner self. You have other cognitive meanings within your cognitive system that you fulfill with your conscious intelligence directly, and all these relate not to your inner world where you reason, learn, and remember, but to your small group of neurons from your prefrontal cortex where you reside, because your actual inner environment as a conscious intelligence spans the few neurons of that small area of the cortex where you reside. And it is only when you form overall ionic membranes that you manage to connect with other areas of the brain and therefore with other cognitive environments. Your third self on your lifeline of existence is the physical body. This exists in this world, and here is where it fulfills all its needs and meanings. You may relate with your organism most of the time, since your senses of perception are placed at its level, and they are in the real world. Even more, the Consensual Matrix with its science and education keeps you in this world, managing to disconnect in every manner all the connections that you have with your other environments, and therefore managing to hide from you the multitude of your selves, which you have everywhere. And this is how you end up failing the multitude of meanings that you were supposed to fulfill throughout life, while focusing the entire time in fulfilling the tasks and duties of the Consensual Matrix, on its behalf.

What meanings exactly? In your inner replica of this world, you have to learn and replicate the outside world accurately, and not through dogma, beliefs, ideals, and fake knowledge and understanding of this world that science and education feed you continuously throughout life. You also have to reason at the intelligent human level through your inner self, in order to be able to fulfill the multitude of your meanings within your cognitive system, within your inner world, within your outer, real world, and within all your higher environments.

We notice that thinking is at the core of your behavior throughout life, and therefore at the core of the fulfillment of all your needs and meanings throughout all your environments. Even more, you should think at the human level, cognitive activity that I call reasoning, or intelligent reasoning. There are four or five forms of thinking, one or more for each developmental level, depending on circumstances. You adopt these forms of thinking throughout life many times without even realizing it, since psychology never teaches you about your own thinking, while the specific form of thinking that you employ makes the difference if you are capable or not to fulfill your needs and meanings throughout life. And this is why, if you remain incapable to fulfill your human meaning, you have to rely on authorities and ideologies of all kind to help you throughout this world. And you may do so just by copying others in what they do and how they fulfill their needs and meanings, or by watching TV, reading books, or searching online.

The zero level thinking relates to disability and addictions. Your zero level meaning in life and in this world is to feel good at all costs and under all circumstances, going against society, Life, and the Divine many times. You still exist in this world at your zero developmental level, but you exist only as an unfavorable environmental condition, and this is why Life is eager to take you out of Existence. And it is only through the intervention of your loved ones that you are still alive at your zero developmental level, because since you cannot fulfill your needs, you cannot subsist, and therefore you die. However, people take drugs in every manner today, legally, illegally, prescribed, and with their food and drinks as additives. While they never die, mostly, and this is the case because they do not take drugs continuously but only in their free time, since they have to go to work and fulfill their needs and meanings in the meantime. And this kills only their private, free life, because they dedicate the rest to the Consensual Matrix.

At the first level thinking, you do everything for your ideologies and hierarchies, everything that they demand from you. Your meaning in life, society, and in this world at the first level is to serve others, doing everything that they want you to do, in the exact manner that they demand, whenever they demand. And if you are a slave or if you are confined in any institution, you will fulfill all your needs and meanings whenever they decide for you to do so. And this is how you eat, drink water, and socialize whenever you are allowed. And this is about all, because they do not allow you to reproduce, learn, and develop while you are confined, and you may not even fulfill your own meanings as a first level being, living your life under oath and servitude. The current consensual, hierarchic Brothers are of the first level, along with soldiers, slaves, servants, adepts, and idealists. The current Brothers still have privileges, and these allow them to fulfill all their needs even better than the Masses. Yet the Brotherhood ideology is very clear, very strong, and very demanding, managing to overtake their human reasoning, managing to replace entirely in this manner their entire human meaning, with whatever their current brotherhood ideology demands from them to do. And it is the same with the invisible kingdom.

While these two, the Brotherhood and the invisible kingdom, decide now the faith of this world with everyone in it. And it is enough for their ideologies to call for the end of this world, and they obey at once, they kill the entire world only to do good in this world, since their ideologies convince them that if they kill this world then they kill all evil in this world, but the entire world will reborn shortly after, from its own ashes. And therefore, they get to save the entire world in this manner, by killing the world, and so they are heroes and saviors. And they do so at once, since the invisible kingdom stands at its core, controlling it tightly.

While the invisible kingdom is different, since the invisible kingdom has its own ideology. And for their ideology, they own and control the current consensual Brotherhood, along with the entire world. It is enough to study this ideology to see how their meaning in life is parasitic in nature, to profit continuously and significantly, and they refer to it as taking tribute. And if they profit one dollar, then they fulfill their meaning in life and in this world, and they are happy and they feel love. However, nobody profits one dollar, because the invisible kingdom owns this world entirely including the Internet and all wars and authorities, and you may see them everywhere.

The invisible kingdom was a real kingdom once, until half a millennium ago, in the Caucasian region, mostly in Georgia. They have nothing to do with Europe and with the holly lands since these two are very far away, yet they have infiltrated these and now they rule the West. While in the East, you have the tyrants and dictators doing the same, while engaging the invisible kingdom. Together they exterminate this world systematically, they already count in tens of millions or probably hundreds of millions by now, they are very successful and very profitable in everything that they do according to their tradition, ideology, and meaning in life and in this world, and soon it will be only their genetic line left.

And even more, it is the invisible kingdom instating the Consensual Matrix on Earth in its current flawless form as you notice it throughout this world. And it seems that this entire matrix that they tend to continuously has a higher being at its top, and this happens to be their direct deity, a deity that also claims to be the true Divine, since all deities have claimed this throughout the ages, and look what they did to this world. And now, this is how their entire objective meaning in life, in society, and in this world, through their deity, becomes a higher meaning in the higher world.

How exactly is everything possible? We have to continue our model for all realities of the wider world, in order to make it apply to all higher beings and higher intelligences of the wider world. Our model can take us that far, since we have all the necessary knowledge in this entire book series, to help us now continue the model of the human meaning covering higher worlds, higher environments, and higher beings.

How sure can you be that higher realities and higher beings exist? Science and education already assure us that this world is the only reality that exists, while religions and spirituality are based on beliefs, and nothing else. And therefore, it is your choice to follow them or not, but in reality, as science and education claim, this world is the only real one, with the big bang to have formed it billions of years ago, and this is the theory. Do higher worlds exist? Because if they do not, then our model ends here, and you already know your meaning in life and in this world in the Consensual Matrix, while there are no Deity, no higher laws, no souls, nothing at all.

Can our entire model assure us that higher worlds exist and they are not only a myth and assumption? No, not at all. Even more, there is nothing in this world assuring us in an accurate, intelligent manner that there are higher worlds and higher beings above our world besides your own faith, higher beings to have created reality and to interact now freely with our world as we dream and reason here in our minds. We may use the beliefs of religion and spirituality in order to help us continue our model now throughout this last chapter, yet this is not intelligent reasoning, but simple ideological thinking. And this is only a first level thinking, related to dogma and servitude. Or even more, we may use inductive reasoning now, to state that, since we may form inner realities through minds and computers here in our world, and since we manage to interact with our inner realities in the exact manner that higher beings interact here in our world as religions and spirituality claim, then these claims must be true, and higher worlds and higher beings truly exist. Therefore, higher realities and higher beings exist, since everything is consistent.

Yet both deductive and inductive reasoning are first level algorithmic reasoning, giving us very little certitude. Because if we cannot be certain through an accurate reasoning and awareness that higher realities and higher beings exist, including souls, higher selves, and holly beings, then we cannot continue our model of the human meaning with this last chapter about higher worlds and higher beings, so we should be happy with what we have found so far.

There is one slight chance to have some assurance throughout this part of the model, and it relates with the highjective nature of existence. Since everything related to higher worlds and higher beings is of a highjective nature in the way we perceive and understand them from our own world. Let us see.

The wider world comprises all realities that exist in any manner, subjectively, highjectively, or objectively, all according to the definition of existence. Even more, all realities of the wider world are of a subjective nature, since the wider world holds them. And for all realities of the wider world, that ultimate reality holding them is of a highjective nature. Therefore, all realities of the wider world are in the same situation as we are here in this last chapter of the book, not being capable to prove accurately that higher realities and higher beings exist, just because these are highjective in nature for them, and therefore they can never tell if their proof is accurate or only inductive. While induction is only a first level algorithmic form of thinking.

What do they do in order to find out the truth? And even more, what if they have higher beings interacting directly with them, to tell them the higher truth? Even then, you can never be certain that what they claim is true, since they may claim anything for any reason, while you must have faith to believe that what they state is true. While faith and beliefs are also of the first, consensual level.

What if higher beings appear directly in their reality, to state through firsthand testimonies that higher beings and higher worlds exist? Higher beings cannot exit and enter realities in their objective form. In order to do so, they have to use avatars to be able to interact with other realities, just as you have your computer characters and inner selves to help you interact with your own inner realities.

And this is why, whenever regular people claim to be extraordinary divinities, it might not be true. They might still be avatars since anyone may be an avatar in this world, everyone may have a soul. And again, if our model proves that higher worlds and higher beings exist, and if it does so not through believes, ideologies, induction, and any lower level thinking, but through intelligent human reasoning, then we may be certain that these exist.

Accurate, intelligent reasoning is based entirely on the natural laws of this universe, as the classical physics and mathematics, while these are part of this world standing at the base of everything from this world, constituting everything that gives meaning to the field, allowing it to shape and reshape everything objective and material in nature that you find everywhere in our world, as far and as long as our world lasts. We have to study our world along with all realities now in every detail relevant to the topic of our model of the human meaning, in order to understand what keeps our model of understanding bounded to this world alone, and to all our inner realities, but not to any of our higher realities, if these even exist.

And as we have seen, existence already states that higher realities and higher beings exist in a highjective form, and therefore in an abstract manner. And this is the problem, because we want our understanding and awareness about our higher environment to be accurate, and not only abstract. We want tangible, objective, substantial, material proof that higher beings and higher environments exist. While objective, substantial, and material existence is capable to define this world, and nothing above, nothing else, just because we use accurate proofs related only to this world and nothing else, since we have nothing else.

Let us see now a brief model of any reality. Again, science

never performs these studies, always remaining constrained to this world in everything that it studies and explains. And even so, it does everything empirically and consensually at the first level. To be more specific, while we base all our accurate, objective research on this world entirely, science bases its research on a first level consensus, the scientific consensus, which happens to remain consistent to the entire Consensual Matrix. Do they do so on purpose?

I am going to state the mathematical definition of a reality now. Mathematics is not exactly another realm, another reality in itself to be able to define them, yet it is a theoretical reality, the only one, mimicking successfully in theory all characteristics of any reality. Using mathematics to define a reality is as using the Carnot engine to define and study all combustion engines in this world, even though the Carnot engine does not really run, it can never be built, and it is not actually an engine, but only a theoretical engine used to define and describe them, theoretically.

Here is the definition of any reality along with its characteristics: a reality is a distinct set of objects and events spanning a commutative topological ring or a commutative topological vector space. A reality might also be a set of more than its continuum, objects, and events, or less, depending on circumstances.

This is a simple definition of a reality, and despite of its apparent simplicity, it includes all characteristics of a reality mentioned throughout my books. In abstract algebra, the words 'commutative,' 'topology,' 'vector space,' and 'rings,' are sufficient to assign to a set or to an entire world the following properties:

The set or reality is continuous, boundless, and it never reaches its limits.

You may never exit or enter any reality in any manner.

You may not go from any point A to any point B of any reality while passing through the outside of that specific reality, or through a gap in reality. Therefore, there are no gaps in any reality and no exit and entering points.

Each reality has its own sets of natural laws and operations defining all criteria of existence of the specific reality.

There always exist null elements and inverse elements within a reality as defined by all internal natural laws and operations specific to that reality.

And these are enough to define realities. Note that these are not beliefs but accurate facts, relating to the natural laws of any reality from their perspective, and you may reason through them in order to apply them to anything you need. If mathematics is too tedious to follow throughout reasoning, we may define realities in a simpler manner:

All realities are objectively real as observed from within, while nothing exists objectively outside them, not even other realities.

You may not assume that other realities do not exist according with their own separate laws of existence.

Realities do not intersect objectively. They do not share information, components, and matrices of continuum in an objective manner.

You may transfer only interpreted copies of objects, subjects, and information between realities, and nothing else.

And this is the problem right here, because you cannot transfer genuine, substantial, accurate information from one reality to another, because this type of accurate, material, objective information may exist only within realities but not at their exterior, since everything objective is held and defined only by that reality alone. And now, all information that we may have about other realities or about our wider world as a whole remains in a personalized copy, which is a belief, it is faith, and this is what religion and spirituality tried to tell us the entire time.

What can we do? We may continue our model with a big assumption here, well motivated. What happens throughout free realities, if these even exist, is that people there may form a consensus that this is always the case, and through their unanimous consensus, they may accept that knowledge about higher worlds is objectively accurate. While this is still consensual and existentially impossible to be real.

Can't we simply talk to these avatars of higher beings to teach us the truth? Just study the majority of religions and schools of thought to find them based on testimonies, knowledge, and teachings of these religious and spiritual characters, all telling us about all higher worlds and higher beings, and everything is found throughout all these ideologies. Or this is what is left of it, because the Consensual Matrix has altered true teachings, if they have ever managed to teach the people significant knowledge, rendering them what you find today. Because even as an avatar of a pertinent higher being, you still transfer through your knowledge only copies of information from one reality to another, and nothing genuine. And even so, these copies of higher knowledge have to be personalized by you, or speculated, in the exact manner that you understand it, as it is filtered through the specific structure of your inner replica of this world. And if your inner replica of this world is altered through beliefs, now this is what you find in all higher worlds, additional beliefs build on beliefs.

Can we simply go to all these higher worlds ourselves, through lucid dreaming, astral projection, and near death experience? Can't we simply die and come back to tell the story, about all souls coming here to Earth, about how they fulfill their needs in this manner, alongside their loved ones that they call soul mates, about their higher environment, and even about our higher meaning in life in everything concerning them and their higher world, place this entire knowledge in our model now, and go on with our study? No, since again, you cannot transfer higher information even in this manner, through you, since you still have to pass from one reality to another and even through your own inner replica of this world. And when you do so, whatever is objective in nature has to remain there since it is not defined elsewhere while you cannot understand it. In other words, you can always understand only through your own mind, reasoning, and inner replica of this world, and these are subjective in nature. And this is how everything highjective becomes subjective, through your own beliefs, theories, speculations, assumptions, and personalization.

It is the same between this world and your inner replica of this world, because you cannot transfer knowledge directly from the real world to your inner replica of this world, but you have to understand it, memorize it, and therefore learn it systematically yourself, transferring in this manner only interpreted copies of knowledge from the outside world to your inner replica of this world.

And what we want to do now is to transfer accurate knowledge from the higher worlds directly into our inner replicas of this world in an accurate manner, just for us to be sure that higher beings, higher worlds, and therefore higher meanings exist accurately. Which already seems impossible, mostly with science and the entire society stating continuously that our world is everything that exists, this life is the only one that we have, and therefore our human meaning is actually the usual consensual duties and tasks that we receive throughout the Consensual Matrix, mostly in the Brotherhood. Enhancing beliefs and obedience.

Which means that, even through lucid dreaming and astral projection to higher worlds, you cannot transfer accurate information from the higher worlds to this world, or from the higher worlds and higher beings to your inner replica of this world. And in this manner, all gurus of this world have only copies of interpreted higher knowledge, regardless of what these may claim. And it is the same with the mediums channeling spirits and higher knowledge in general, everything is copied, interpreted knowledge, but not accurate knowledge.

While we can maintain accuracy only with this world and with the cognitive inner worlds of this world, through the natural laws of this world, and through all the accurate objects, subjects, events, words, definitions of words, and lines and lifelines of causality of this world and of the inner cognitive worlds of this world. As your inner replica of this world.

Yet even so, this does not mean that this world is the supreme, ultimate world or reality as science claims, with the living human beings as the supreme, most developed living beings in the universe, just because absence of proof does not mean proof of absence of higher worlds, higher beings, and higher circumstances. While it is not accurate for science to state that this world is the ultimate world, and that this life is the only one that you have.

Furthermore, just as you learn normally by transferring interpreted copies of information from the outside world to your inner replica of this world, you do so along your own lifeline of existence, since you have your inner self and your outer self on your lifeline of existence, and therefore you may interact in the two worlds simultaneously while transferring information, through you.

It is the same while learning higher knowledge from higher worlds, because you have to do so through your own lifeline of existence, if you have your selves there. Which is possible through your souls, yet it is possible for them and not for you the living human being, since they precede you on your lifeline of existence. They have you, but you do not have them.

Your other option is to lucid dream or project, but even so, you lucid dream and project through your higher selves, since you have to have one already there in order to lucid dream or project there. Try it, to see it for yourself.

You may try even tonight when you go to bed, to go, project, and reach these higher realities yourself, just to experience for yourself how the objective knowledge is limited to the specific reality defining it, and nothing more. This gives distinction, individuality, and uniqueness to every reality, and this is why realities last as long and as far as they exist, objectively. While the One or the wider world lasts and exists as far and as long as everything within exists in all existential natures, and not only objectively.

For example, when you reach higher astral and etheric realities, you may meet important religious characters there, or you may meet the Divine Himself, along with Life and Intelligence, if you have the chance. You may even talk with them in order to find out more about your true meaning in this world and in the higher world, along with what life is. While they will give you exactly the list of meanings that I stated in the beginning of the book, in very beautiful words and teachings, uplifting you. There are people who even met Santa Claus right after meeting wonderful religious characters and the Divine Himself, as they even got to speak with Santa Claus, just because their specific inner understanding and replica of this world allowed it. And then they probably went to meet Batman and Spiderman since they are in astral planes, and this made for an extraordinary dream, lucid dream, or astral projection.

Because many astral planes and etheric planes are summations of everything ever happening everywhere, not in the exact manner it happened, but in the exact manner that people think, know, remember, and believe that it happened. This is exactly objective accuracy for the etheric plane with its entire Akashi records, since the etheric plane contains all facts and beliefs from here from this world, exactly as these come from everyone. While here in this world, many beliefs are not accurate, but only consensual, or even fictional, as Batman himself.

There are still astral planes holding only truths, yet you cannot understand them once you came back to our world, since all understanding implies the use of your mind, reasoning, and inner replica of this world, and these are subjective even to this world. In other words, you cannot perceive and understand higher worlds and higher beings through your own reasoning in your inner replica of this world, as accurate as it might be, since it is of a lower existential level. You are of a lower existential level entirely, along with this entire world.

Therefore, in everything concerning higher worlds and higher beings, you have to use your own higher selves or souls found on your own lifeline of existence. But these are not your own reasoning, judgment, and knowledge anymore, but theirs, your souls'. While as seen, they precede you on your lifeline of existence, and you can never be them. Just as Mario cannot be you, to play you here in our world, but it is only the other way around, you become Mario and you play him in the computer inner world.

Yet there is a way out of this entire higher circumstance related to your higher human meaning. Your higher human meaning is not exactly yours as a living human being, but it is your soul's. If you have a soul. Because if you do not have a soul, then problem solved. Your problem is solved not only regarding your higher meaning, higher knowledge, higher learning, and higher behavior, but regarding religion and spirituality just as well.

But do you have a soul? And how can you ever know? Some souls actually come in this world to live life in first person, directly as souls, and not as living human beings. While other souls come here only in third person, allowing you in this manner to exist as a living human being in parallel with it. Which is just as common. Yet you may also share your entire highconscious main intelligence with your soul. Which means that you are both the soul and the living human being, always thinking, feeling, and experiencing the same thing throughout this life. In which case, you cannot even know that you have a soul, since its own cognition is glued to yours. While your soul does not know that it is actually a soul and not the living human being, since its cognition is glued to yours, it is the same main highconscious intelligence of your mind.

And this is how all your higher meaning in Life and in the wider world belongs to your higher selves, as many and as high you have them on your own lifeline of existence. What you can still do, you may always be careful to fulfill their own higher needs and higher meanings here in this world, while never standing in their way while they fulfill their own higher needs and higher meanings just as well. Because a bottle of vodka will go a long way, to corrupt them and compromise their own higher meanings. Because you are the gardener of your own soul, and you should always consider it. Or you are the soul altogether, affecting you longer.

Can we actually know what they know? Can we know all

higher knowledge ourselves, through our own mind, reasoning, awareness, and understanding? What ideologies including spirituality do here, they use consensual beliefs in order to define higher knowledge themselves, and this is an even lower form of reasoning, consensual in nature. Yet there are other ways to know more higher knowledge accurately, by all higher laws, through all human higher circumstances, while you have to consider all human limitations and errors of reasoning, since these stand in your way.

As a reference, you happen to dream and experience significantly more throughout your dreams every night, only that you cannot remember everything, but you can remember only what relates to your own understanding about this world when you wake up, to your own inner replica of this world. And this is the case just because you dream through various other selves of yourself, inner and higher, even through your soul and the souls of your soul. Everything is firsthand, objective, consistent, accurate knowledge and experience that you have throughout higher worlds, only that it is impossible for you to remember, to bring it here in this world when you wake up, because you lack your own knowledge and understanding of everything that you have learned and experienced at a higher level through your higher mind, and therefore you do not have the words and concepts to remember and understand it here in this world.

It is different with our inner realities, because we create them through our knowledge and understanding, and therefore everything happening in there remains consistent with everything that we are capable to understand up here, and we can know everything. You still cannot transfer objects and subjects to and from mind and computer realities, but at least you are capable to transfer most of the knowledge and meanings. And it is the same with souls, since they are capable to remember full experiences that they have here, they learn through them, and they are capable to fulfill their developmental needs and meanings through them here in this world. And then, whenever their avatars start talking about other higher realms and everything happening there, everything has to be true, at least as much and as far as these avatars are capable to understand, correlate, and remember. And even so, how exactly can you be sure that they are telling the truth, now after selling the entire story to movie producers for profit?

What we can do in this circumstance is to gather all consistent higher knowledge from all sources: religion, spirituality, old records of higher knowledge, along with millions of testimonies from people who traveled in every manner to these higher worlds and learned the truth. We use only the most consistent knowledge, and this is about the best that anyone can do here in this world and in other realities in order to find higher truth. There is another way, if you are actually a soul living life firsthand here on Earth, remembering everything from your higher world. Since now, you may tell the truth to everyone to hear clearly, everything that happens in your higher world. You may be on TV, on websites, you may write books, or make videos. They will never let you on mainstream TV, yet you can post videos on social media, make websites and write books, since everything is possible. And in this manner, you are part of the millions of testimonies that we consider.

While as stated, the human reasoning has a higher side, just because the human mind is divided in the conscious, subconscious, and highconscious main intelligences. Your highconscious main intelligence always relates and remains connected to the higher self. Therefore, we use firsthand awareness and reasoning throughout this research continuously, and this may remain objective in nature if we only follow all rules meant to assure the pertinence of any third level research and reasoning.

What exactly are these rules assuring pertinent intelligent research and reasoning? I use these throughout all research, and this is why all books of this series remain consistent. First, for an accurate, intelligent reasoning, you have to avoid all lower level knowledge, as knowledge coming from empiric research, beliefs, and simple algorithmic thinking, because these may be empirical and therefore misleading if it happens to be erroneous, compromising your research. It is only at the end when you see how similar your results are, compared to what religions and schools of thought already state through their beliefs, but there are millions of beliefs of all nature throughout this world, and you can never tell what is relevant and what is not.

Secondly, you have to avoid empiric research. Empiric research is significantly easier to perform, since you may simply observe your subject of study, and then you may use all appearances in order to invent anything that you can or please as an explanation, and this may be true or not. As a reference, all current theories invented by science are empiric, including the theory of relativity, the big bang theory, the theory of evolution, along with many theories from quantum mechanics and the rest of the modern physics. And even more, since science cannot feed inaccurate knowledge to the people, science labels these with the word 'theory' in their title, and this means that nothing stated there is actually accurate but only a theory, assumption, or speculation, anything that scientists thought about it whenever they researched it. This may be true or false, and this is how science is always legitimate, since it defines its own laws, in a major conflict of interest. And if the people want to believe it as an accurate fact, then they may certainly do so. And again, you notice your own consensus to participate in all lies of science, and nothing else. Yet you can never find and keep a job as a scientist if you do not agree to this consensual scientific consensus. And without being part of science, you do not exist in the genuine world of science today, just because science monopolizes this world of genuine science today.

And this is the case with medicine, education, finance, entertainment, and academia, since these are monopolies taking over their entire domain, while nobody notices. While none are true, but only consensuses, only ideologies and propagated beliefs, but not accurate facts. And when it happens in science, it only dumbs you down. But when it happens in medicine, it kills you. When it happens in education, it indoctrinates you for life. And when it happens in finance, it ruins you.

And coincidentally, the invisible kingdom owns all these domains, along with much more in this world, or along with the entire world. Because the Consensual Matrix allows them to take possession of the entire world in this manner, their own ideology allows them to employ the Consensual Matrix and harm and exploit this world in every manner, while exterminating everyone else.

A third requirement for an accurate intelligent research is to stay out of loops of reasoning. Because if you do not stay out of all loops of reasoning, then you may state anything about other realities and about higher beings, since you can never know the exact truth about them. And this is how you may get to open your own cult, religion, or school of thought, and no one will ever prove you wrong, because they too cannot bring accurate knowledge about higher worlds here in our world. Similarly, science may state anything it wants about what happened at the time of the assumed big bang, since you were never there to witness it. And now you learn about quantum physics, string theories, and universes of sixteen dimensions found everywhere while you can never prove these wrong either. Even more, since you can never go past the lower orbit of Earth, you can never know how Earth looks like from up there, flat or spherical. And since space missions never go there either, despite of what they may claim, you can never prove them right or wrong, and these are good examples of loops of reasoning. What I found throughout my research is that you may fall into loops of reasoning every time you attempt to define systems as a whole, with the causality itself changing direction when you do so.

And another thing that you have to consider throughout intelligent reasoning and research is the entire line of causality related to your subject in study. Empirical research will study only the consequence, the result, inventing anything as a cause. Cosmologists observe the redshift phenomenon today along with the background radiation, to match them now with the big bang as a main cause. And since they are already in a loop of reasoning because you can never go and be there to witness the big bang for yourself and prove them wrong, now they get away with it. And so they end up indoctrinating this world, since the observed redshift and background radiation have their causes in entirely different events. Because accurate intelligent research follows the entire line of causality throughout the study. And since every meaningful research topic may teach humans anything necessary for their development, everything is done on purpose for scientific research to fail, only not to allow pertinent knowledge to reach this world.

All accurate intelligent study must base itself on the natural laws of this world, the natural laws defining our world, as classical physics and mathematics, since these are capable to define in an accurate manner everything here in our world. While as already stated, everything found in this manner is already part of this world, but not part of the higher worlds and realities. You may use the higher laws for a higher accuracy, and again, you have to do so through all higher selves of your lifeline of existence and through their own higher reasoning, as high as you have them throughout the wider world. If you have any, since the Brothers are taught today that they do not have souls. Which can always be true, since look what they do to this world. Because once you lack souls, it is assumed that you lack higher meaning, along with higher responsibility. And it is assumed in this manner that you lack care just as well, and therefore you should be more willing to harm this world, now without a soul. And if this makes any sense to you, then the current consensual Brotherhood and the entire Consensual Matrix want you for sure, along with all your souls and their higher abilities, since this is the purpose of the entire Consensual Matrix on Earth and in the wider world.

Everything that you research must remain consistent. And when it happens that it loses consistency, you have to find out why. In our case, whatever we model in this chapter will remain consistent with this book and book series, and will remain consistent with other sources, as religions, schools of thought, old records, and firsthand testimonies, not with individuals, but with their entire consistency, with what makes them similar and consistent. And even so, since we consider highjective knowledge, there is nothing allowing us to prove its objective, substantial proof.

And this is how we are going to continue our model now in the highjective side of the human meaning, by maintaining a very careful and very accurate intelligent research, by maintaining a very careful consistency with the rest of the model of the human meaning and with the rest of this book series, by maintaining a close consistency with all relevant sources and records, mostly with those left untouched by the Consensual Matrix, and what is more important, by expanding all lines of causality from this book and from this entire book series to cover this last part of the model of the human meaning. This still includes inductive algorithmic thinking of a lower level, yet with all these considered, it is everything that we may do. While the souls can certainly do a better job, but only as far as their own existential level can take them. And from there, they have to do what we do, in order to know and understand even higher truth, up to Life, Intelligence, Interconnectivity, and the Divine, who know everything there is, just as spirituality states the entire time.

And even so, there is nothing objective to prove in this last part of our model, because nothing can ever prove in an objective manner that other realities and living beings exist above our world, but only highjectively. Our research is not of a first level in this manner, empirical, ideological, or algorithmic, but it is still analytic in nature, only that it is not objectively analytic as we are used to do throughout this book series, but it is highjectively analytic, as this is still a third level research and reasoning, while attempting to be more. And now we are ready to continue the model of the human higher meaning.

We have already noticed that the higher human meaning is

not exactly the human meaning, but it is the meaning of your soul. While everything that you do here on Earth affects your soul, positively or negatively. And in general, if your soul is human in the higher world, then you even maintain correspondence.

Our model for the human meaning is always the same: you have a multitude of selves, and through them, you live your life within a multitude of environments, many times simultaneously, along your own lifeline of existence. And throughout all these environments, you may fulfill your needs, while you always have to fulfill your meaning or meanings, in the exact manner that you receive them from the multitude of specialized intelligences of your cognitive system. What we have also noticed is that you may have a multitude of environments that you may occupy through the same self, all depending on the existential nature of the respective reality where you exist, within your cognitive system, which is an inner reality having a subjective existential nature.

You may have a multitude of environments of a subjective nature as seen from the perspective of this world. And this is how you have several environments there, as the small area of the cortex that you inhabit as an intelligent inner self offering you a specific intelligent meaning, along with your inner replica of this world where you have the multitude of cognitive meanings to tend to as an intelligent inner self, as seen above. Your human meaning is in the outside world, in this world, where you live your life as a living human being. In the intelligent human society, you should have your social self, who has its own genuine social meanings, yet the current human society is dead, consensually dead. Since this is how you have ended up with a consensual self in the current human society, which is your trademark, brand, or consensual corporation. And this is how you live your life most of the time, through your consensual corporation, or as a consensual corporation, assuming that you are a living human being the entire time.

It is the same in the outside world, where you have a

multitude of environments to tend to through specialized or generalized tasks as needed, and these are your natural environment made of pristine forests and lakes, along with your built environment made of apartment buildings, roads, and factories, along with your family environment, work and school environments, community environment, nation environment, society environment, and many more. While in all these, you have a specialized or generalized task to fulfill, through your physical body this time.

What adds to our research now is the fact that existence has three natures: subjective, objective, and highjective. While so far, throughout the research, we have covered only your subjective and objective selves, environments, and meanings. End even so, we would still not have to add higher selves, higher environments, and higher meanings to our research of the human meaning, if only for the fact that you interact continuously with higher environments throughout the day, through a multitude of higher selves of your lifeline of existence, even simultaneously, while fulfilling higher tasks and meanings the entire time, as all these might be relevant to know and consider.

How exactly do you do so? How do you get to exit this world while nothing can enter or exit it in its current form? You do so through your avatars, or higher and lower selves of your own lifeline of existence. Your conscious intelligence and your inner selves do so continuously, since they are not of this world, but they are of the lower realities of your cognitive system. While you manage to exit toward higher realities in a similar manner, having this time your physical body as an inner self as seen from higher perspectives, inner self living in this world, which is only an inner replica of a higher reality, found only in someone's mind, since everything has a cognitive meaning, and not a technological one. Which means that our world is still natural even though it is created, very similar with the multitude of inner cognitive worlds of your mind that you create continuously throughout your reasoning, in order to provide a proper environment for all your inner intelligences to perform their acts and mental models on your behalf, and then to offer you the final idea, as successful as you expect it.

But how do you exit this world, even when you do so through your higher self? Do you simply fly away, as explained by spirituality? No, not at all, since the movement of flying implies remaining within the same reality, while projecting involves switching from one reality to another. And you cannot do so directly through your conscious self, but you have to do so through your higher self. And this is why you always have to lose consciousness in order to do so, as you do when you fall asleep, when you have a traumatic experience, when you take psychotropic substances, or when you die, because you have to be able to switch selves and therefore project to their own environments, worlds, and realities. You already do so with the multitude of your inner selves throughout your mind, yet you manage to keep consciousness, since your consciousness happens to be subjective in nature, standing below you on your lifeline of existence as a conscious intelligence. And even so, even within your cognitive system, you are not the only one thinking, but you have a multitude of intelligences helping you throughout your reasoning. Many may reason just as accurately as you do, only that you can never access their consciousness to witness it. They perform a multitude of mental models throughout the multitude of their inner worlds, some specialized and some not, some created by them as a direct replica of this world while some use your own inner replica of this world as a model, or an even lower inner replica of this world as a model, making copies after copies in this manner depending on the existential level that they inhabit within your cognitive system. And after all reasoning and mental modeling, they serve you a multitude of ideas for you to choose now, and this is how you reason. And it is you creating all these mind realities, zillions in number, while you and others alike have entire selves above to have created this entire world. You live here now through your physical body while you also live up there through your higher bodies, higher selves, and higher worlds, and everything is consistent.

And now when you ask how you manage to exit this world and go to higher worlds, it is simply because you are by far more complex and more meaningful than entire worlds and realities. This is what the Consensual Matrix tries to hide from you the entire time, this is why science never leaves this world throughout its research, this is why you have to take medicine, vaccines, and food additives in order to remain disconnected from your higher selves, and this is why you have to be stopped from fulfilling your higher needs and meanings, because they might try to develop you and the entire world to your intelligent human level, and all these open your awareness toward higher worlds. And if psychology asks you questions as do you hear voices in your head, or do you see things that are not there, it only does so in order to make sure that you are still disabled, still as a lower self, and still in your lower environments. Here you are more complex, more meaningful, and more important than entire worlds and realities, while the Consensual Matrix keeps you confined and entirely disabled only to be able to milk your higher abilities, compromising your entire existence in the process. Because you do not exactly go to higher worlds at night while you reason, while you project, and when you die, but you simply choose and switch yourself from one of your own realities to another, to be aware there. Because you already exist there through all selves of your lifeline of existence, as you exist everywhere else, in all your realities.

And it is only because of this highjective existence that we have now to add this entire chapter of our model of the human meaning, in order to study your higher meaning. And we do so by considering your highconscious mind or highjective intelligence within your cognitive system, alongside your conscious and subconscious intelligences. Your highjective intelligence and therefore the highconscious part of your mind is not here in this world since it is highjective in nature, but it is part of higher realities, and everything is consistent with your subconscious intelligence or subjective part of your mind which is not in this world either, but it is an inner world in an inner cognitive reality. And this is only a simplistic model of your cognitive system, since you have higher and higher selves and minds on top of these alongside your lifeline of existence, just as you have lower and lower cognitive realities within your mind holding inner, inner intelligences, as far down your existential lifeline as your specific cognitive activity requires.

Note that our world is always real and even objective in nature, since all realities are objective in nature as long as you are there to witness. Because from upper perspectives, everything seems subjective in there, while from lower perspectives, everything appears to be highjective in nature here.

How exactly do higher worlds and higher beings look like? Everything is correspondent. They look exactly as close or as different than you, as your inner self looks closer or different than you the living human being. And about higher worlds, they should look just as what is and happens here in our world, only in a more complex and more detailed form and meaning, just because replicas of replicas tend to lose details and even cognitive resolution. Or this is the case if our world is created in the image of our higher reality, which seems to be the case according to most of the sources. And even more, since you are part of this world, you cannot see the 'pixels' from within our world, just because you are part of everything and not of the missing details. And this is why everything that you perceive and experience has all details in place and does not miss a spot, a detail, or an object. And this is the case just because everything that you know here consciously you know it from there, from the real world. And you can never know what you do not know in order to compare it with what you know, to help you learn the difference between this world and its higher counterpart. Again, through inductive reasoning, you may start drawing or painting, and the difference between what you draw and the real world is exactly the difference between the real world and our higher reality.

Yet there are exceptions to this reasoning, because small discrepancies will always appear in the real world, and you will never know why, but you will only wonder. As it is the case with little changes not in your inner replica of this world because these happen continuously throughout life and it does not amaze you anymore, as when you happen to forget something, but when these cognitive mistakes happen directly in the outside world, affecting specific details there, which are missing sometimes, or which are entirely different, and it makes you wonder. This is called Mandela Effect. And sometimes, it might have to do with the way this world is held, formed, and maintained in the upper reality.

Many people were puzzled to find out from the news that Mandela finally was released from prison, while he had actually died in prison years before, and it had been such a dreadful, tragic event. He had been buried, and it was such an impressive funeral service. And this got everybody puzzled.

However, this world is not created the way you create your inner replica of this world throughout life, just because you happen to live your life disconnected throughout life. And as stated throughout this book, intelligences live life together, within entire cognitive systems. While you as a conscious intelligence are always alone in your own mind. Even animals live life together within their mind, and this is why animals do not have to use words in order to talk. But animals are stupid, science states, and this is why they cannot communicate. While now, if I state here that animals are able to communicate, just as humans do, and they do so in a telepathic manner, I enter one of those loops of reasoning stated before, just because I can never prove that I am right. While you can never prove that I am wrong. Yet all animals communicate at their own second intuitive level, telepathically or not, lacking intelligent concepts.

What I have noticed is that humans are capable to teach primates sign language, and in this manner, primates are capable to communicate with humans even through abstract conceptual information. I watched these conversations with animals in a multitude of videos. Animals used sign language to communicate with humans, but never among themselves.

While they always knew everything about the other animals in the group, even complex, abstract knowledge, without using sign language among themselves. And everything relates with interconnectivity, since you are made to live your life disabled, cognitively disconnected from the rest of this world, only to keep you unaware of what happens to you throughout life in this world.

Yet higher selves still use higher cognitive abilities, allowing them to remain connected throughout life at least within their higher world. This is how they behave, telepathically, and this is how they reason and learn, telepathically.

How exactly would your own inner replica of this world look like, if you were a telepath yourself? How would you live your family life as a telepath? And without the Consensual Matrix instated, if you had access to a family as large as an entire community or city, how exactly would you live your life there, where you do not have only one spouse and they do not have only you as a spouse, where the idea of having designated spouses would not even make sense, then how exactly would you interact with everybody from your overall family? Are these possible, or these are only utopic questions? Yet how can they be utopic, when the idea itself of having only one spouse throughout life is utopic in itself? It is enforced by law, and it goes against your human nature. Because if your reproductive intelligence has reacted immediately, and now it sends you several needs at once to get you well prepared for all these overall human families, does this not mean that there is an accurate human meaning related to them, to go there or to make you modify your current environment into that? Meaning that wants you to go into those intelligent human families filled with telepaths and where you do not have to claim spouses but where you may interact as you please, and have as many friends as you please, within an overall family. And if you ever want to leave to be with other families, you may do so at once, you may travel all over this world to be with all overall families if you please, since you are always accepted, since this is your choice.

And if the Consensual Matrix was not instated, and if you

had all your higher abilities and all your human rights respected, how exactly would you behave? What would you do? What would be your meaning in life and in this world then? How would you reason? How would you communicate? Would you simply find anyone and start exchanging one word after another in your mind, so you can talk in this manner for some time, just as you do through sounds? Would you use pictures instead, in order to recall a movie that you have once seen, and he or she would watch the pictures while following your words in your mind describing the entire movie? Or would you be able to transfer the dialogue, telepathically, and now he or she can watch the entire movie normally, from your mind, without having to download it form the Internet? No, not at all, none of these would be the case in a community of telepaths, since the common human mind is significantly more capable. It is the same at school. Would the teacher stand in front of the students in order to tell the class directly in their mind the entire lesson? No, not at all. But how exactly would people talk on the phone, do their job, buy things, invent things, and visit the bathroom, if they are telepaths? Because this is exactly the topic of this book, what is your meaning in a free world where you still have all your cognitive abilities intact? What exactly would you do? This is exactly as asking how you walk to the store now when you take the car. Will you still have to wear shoes? Because it is an entire different circumstance within communities of telepaths, and we have to study it carefully in its own context exactly as it takes place, but never empirically, as it might seem normal to happen from here, from the current consensual, dilapidated, handicapped human social and environmental context, as you notice throughout movies.

There are many human higher abilities besides telepathy, and I study them in a separate book of this series. Free communities of telepaths do not have to use words, secrets, and pictures, but are capable to create a common inner replica of this world just as accurate or just as customized as they want, yet always remaining relatively identical with the outside world. Because everything that we do in life we do to fulfill needs and meanings, while all these needs and meanings remain consistent with the outside world, or at least with a consensual outside world. And so this commune, telepathic inner replica of the outside world remains relatively similar to the outside world, having all adjustments in place just as everybody desires, which is, just as primal intelligences send them needs to adjust it, and so they do. And you might not get to see the Consensual Matrix present in there, since no one might need to have the Consensual Matrix in their own private world. Do you have the Consensual Matrix at home in the family? Yet you always take the Consensual Matrix with you wherever you go if you live your life underdeveloped. Yet developed communities of telepaths might be the first genuine free human communities.

Since this is the meaning of having a common inner replica of this world, in order to be able to fulfill your needs and meanings undisturbed, as efficiently as possible. You still have to fulfill your physiological needs in the outside world as eating, recovery, and breathing, yet you may fulfill all these while still living your life in the common inner replica of this world, undisturbed. And this example is highly significant to research now, because that higher inner common replica of this world is this world. With all higher telepaths as our own souls from our own lifelines of existence, and with us their avatars here on Earth.

We have found the higher meaning of creating this kind of realities as this world, which is to fulfill higher level needs and meanings. While what you are more interested in, is how to behave now in a world that is simply created by a group of people somewhere in a higher world. Since this is your higher human meaning. You have to know your role first as an avatar in this inner world. You could be the inner self of anyone from above, in which case, that higher being is your higher self, integral part of your cognitive system and lifeline of existence, simply reasoning and daydreaming throughout your real world, through you. Therefore, your higher meaning in this circumstance is to behave normally and naturally, just as you already do.

Another circumstance is that you are not a direct avatar of any of the higher beings, but you are simply a replica of anyone from the higher world that is not present there, or that is not present there right then. And this is always the case in your own inner world, since all replicas of everyone around from your inner world lacks direct interconnectivity with its counterpart from this world. What always happens in your own inner replica of this world is that all replicas of all those around are ready to behave normally and freely under any circumstance that you are ready to simulate in your mind throughout your reasoning.

As a free character in the common inner replica of this world, you do not have a soul or higher self, but you are simply created as an independent inner being by the higher selves together, as part of the scene, and therefore you may behave freely and naturally. Because if you behave consensually for any reason, it might go against the meaning that they had expected from you when they had created you.

You may want to know if you can do anything that you please in a world where you were created for a specific reason, and if you must know that reason too in order to behave according to your creator. Yet you are already fulfilling your meaning, by living your life naturally, according to your own inner needs and meanings. This is why you have a choice. Even more, there are countless of people and entities trying to convince you to do otherwise, and implicitly to start serving them. And this is how people are indoctrinated and fall into servitude, drifting apart from Life and the Divine. And it happens with everybody throughout the Consensual Matrix, since the Consensual Matrix entirely is not part of Life and the Divine, but it is dead, consensually dead.

Do you have or not a soul or higher self? You always have a higher self, by default, since your cognitive system cannot function otherwise. However, you might have or not have an actual soul, depending on circumstances. How can you tell? It is always different. Some souls act on you in first person mode, and others in third person mode. Some only watch you and learn, some intervene in different circumstances, some want you to be aware of their presence, some want you unaware and therefore as natural as possible. And it is always easy to tell. If there are 'miracles' around sometimes, which is, if you feel higher intervention in your life, then be sure that you have a soul, always caring for you. Or if you feel continuous higher love, mostly when you fulfill needs and meanings related to higher knowledge, or if you are very creative, if you show higher abilities at times, if you are a subject of continuous attack from the Consensual Matrix, if you avoid the Consensual Matrix in everything that you do, if you are very interested in art, and more importantly, if you can feel art and if you are capable to distinguish genuine art from the ordinary, then you certainly have a soul, just because art is the entertainment of the soul, and you can always create and understand it through your soul.

What is your higher meaning now? Just behave normally and naturally, as a living human being. You do not have to perform rituals and you do not have to sacrifice anything, just behave normally. Just cooperate with your higher self or soul, just as you cooperate with your other intelligences of your cognitive system or with your family at home and with your friends and colleagues in society. Maintain both inner and higher harmony, and what is very important, whatever you do, try not to harm your soul. As stated previously, medicine, vaccines, food additives, and drugs will harm your higher self and soul so much, that it might abandon you, or destroy you, or drive you mad. While through all these drugs, you might even kill your soul. Autistic people have it the worst, since their medication is designed to kill souls. However, the specific additives that you find in milk and cookies in North America are just as harmful, along with additives in vaccines and baby food from jars, along with additives found in juices and canned food, mostly in everything made for children.

How exactly can your higher self ever abandon you, if it is

part of your cognitive system? Because the example with the community of telepaths is too simplistic compared to what you find happening throughout the higher worlds. And as you may already notice, this world is not exactly created normally in order to engage in intelligent reasoning, but to provide entertainment, social media, and casual subjective lifestyle. And it is through its roughness and relative dangerous circumstances that souls choose it, for its relative popularity, and for the common knowledge and training that you may always have out of this entire experience as a soul.

What exactly is different from this simplistic example? Firstly, it takes a large community of billions of people to make this world possible. Secondly, in order for this world to have achieved this degree of detailed stability, density, and amazing accuracy and consistency in everything, it means that it is a relatively old world, with souls coming and leaving continuously, participating in all experiences, while adding something to this world, something different and personal. And this is how this world looks and behaves now, probably with the initial groups of telepaths long gone by now. And this is how, if you have a soul, then your soul had to get on top of your own higher self in order to come here, since the initial telepaths might be gone by now.

Why possession and what is wrong with it? Nothing, only that not all souls are alike, while not all souls prefer similar avatars. Some are nice or rough, others have more in common with the human species, while others might be significantly different. While it seems that there are reptilian species as souls, and they had been here for a very long time. Some like it here and some do not. Many times, they act together in order to obtain whatever they want, as some tend to be discriminatory. And there are other details, because some souls can stand food additives while others die or are repelled, some can stand even radiation, others are attracted to violence, wars, and disasters, others like bullying and trolling, others are good souls, some want to develop you, to raise you nicely and give you a beautiful personality, others want you rough in life in order to succeed. Some like continuous pleasure, while others want to help this world through you. Many souls like higher art and higher achievement, but they are gone now, repelled by the entire consensual everywhere, so they took all higher beauty with them, away from this world.

The End

ABOUT THE AUTHOR

Valentin Leonard Matcas, M.Ed., is a researcher, physicist, mathematician, educator, and an author of nonfiction and fiction books, including the entire "Human" book series. Valentin Leonard Matcas wrote the "Human" book series in the following order: "The Human Needs", "The Human Addictions," "The Hierarchy of Needs," "Stay in Shape, Lead a Healthy Life," "The Human Origins," "The Human Society," "The Human Conspiracy," "The Human Mind," "The Human Reality," "Astral Planes and Your Other Realities," "Life," "The Hierarchy of Intelligences," "The Human Intelligences," "The Human Thoughts," "Mental Models and Successful Ideas," "The Human Attitudes," "The Human Stereotypes," "The Human Ideology," "Modes of Life," "The Human Development," "Patterns of Development," "The Human Lifestyle," "Heal Yourself," "The Human Civilization," "The Human Religion and Spirituality," "The Human Rights," "Higher Laws," "Natural Laws of the Universe," "Existence," "The Human Condition", "Lifelines of Causality," "The Human Behavior," "Flat Earth," "The Human Environment," "The Human Meaning," "The Human Reasoning," "The Human Interconnectivity," "The Consensual Matrix," "The Matrix of Life," and "The Human Knowledge." Valentin Leonard Matcas writes about terrestrial and alien civilizations, about life in the universe, the way it develops and intertwines across galaxies, about powerful beings as they control and reshape the universe, and about normal living human beings from Earth caught in this beautiful, wider, outstanding interconnectivity. Valentin Leonard Matcas creates a living, warmer universe in his books, teaming with life and vibrancy, on all levels of existence. Valentin Leonard Matcas also wrote "The Storyteller" book series, including "The Storyteller," "Starship Colonial," and "Unlimited," and "The Culling" book series, including "The Culling," "The Dream of the Dead," and "The Last Man on Earth."

When he does not work on his books, Valentin Leonard Matcas enjoys researching, hiking, swimming, kayaking, skiing, snowboarding, biking, reading, listening to music, and playing strategy videogames. You may discover all his books, videos, and articles.